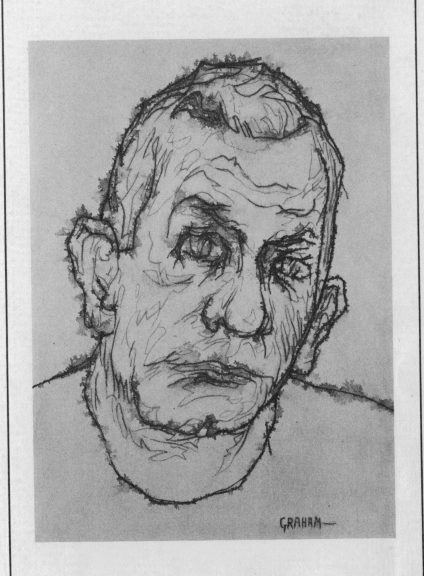

GRAHAM—

STEINBECK: The Man and His Work

STEINBECK:

The Man and His Work

Proceedings of the 1970 Steinbeck Conference

Sponsored by SAN DIEGO PUBLIC LIBRARY

Oregon State and Ball State Universities

Edited by

Richard Astro and Tetsumaro Hayashi

Corvallis:

OREGON STATE UNIVERSITY PRESS

The Executors of the Estate of John Steinbeck have approved this publication.

The Viking Press, Inc., has granted permission to quote from the following works of John Steinbeck: *In Dubious Battle* © 1936, renewed 1964 by John Steinbeck; *Tortilla Flat* © 1935, renewed 1963 by John Steinbeck; *The Long Valley* © 1938, renewed 1966 by John Steinbeck; *Of Mice and Men* © 1937, renewed by John Steinbeck; *Cup of Gold* © 1929 by Robert M. McBride & Company, 1936 by John Steinbeck, and 1957 by John Steinbeck; *To a God Unknown* © 1933, renewed by John Steinbeck; *The Log from the Sea of Cortez* © 1941 by John Steinbeck and Edward F. Ricketts, 1951 by John Steinbeck, renewed 1969 by John Steinbeck and Edward F. Ricketts, Jr.; *The Grapes of Wrath* © 1939, renewed 1967 by John Steinbeck; *Cannery Row* © 1945 by John Steinbeck; *The Wayward Bus* © 1947 by John Steinbeck; *Sweet Thursday* © 1954 by John Steinbeck; *Journal of a Novel* © 1969 by the Executors of the Estate of John Steinbeck.

THE JOHN STEINBECK SOCIETY

IT IS MY PRIVILEGE to extend the greetings of the John Steinbeck Society (1966-   ) and the editorial staff of the *Steinbeck Quarterly* (1968-   ). As director of the society and editor of the three-year old journal, I would like to describe some of the most important functions of the society and the quarterly. In 1966 Preston Beyer, America's prominent Steinbeck collector, and I founded the Steinbeck Bibliographical Society, which became the John Steinbeck Society in 1969, in order to exchange information pertaining to all primary and secondary materials of Steinbeck; soon after that, however, we began to feel that our service should exceed that of merely exchanging bibliographical information. With the participation of Professor Robert DeMott, then at Kent State University, we began in 1968 to issue in mimeograph form the *Steinbeck Newsletter,* in which we published articles, book reviews, dissertation abstracts, a book exchange column, a membership directory, and an annual bibliography. With the enthusiastic financial and administrative support of Ball State University, under the leadership of Dr. Robert L. Carmin, Dean of the College of Sciences and Humanities, and Dr. Thomas H. Wetmore, then Chairman of the English Department, we began to print the *Steinbeck Newsletter* commercially in the spring of 1968. Beginning with the Fall 1969 issue, the journal was renamed the *Steinbeck Quarterly.* A number of people—college professors, high school teachers, librarians, book sellers, book collectors, air force officers, housewives, government officials, business executives, and lawyers, who literally represents all walks of life, began to join us as active members in 1968. Today we have memberships in eight countries: the United States, Japan, Canada, England, Germany, India, Malaysia, and Korea.

Such enthusiasm unmistakably reveals the popularity of John Steinbeck and his works among the most heterogeneous groups of people in spite of the bitter criticism he has received from academic circles and New York critics. Therefore, the functions of the John Steinbeck Society have become increasingly demanding. Some of the most important services we now are extending to our members and other Steinbeckians are:

✔ To publish the *Steinbeck Quarterly* (Winter, Spring, Summer, and Fall issues);

✔ To publish the Steinbeck Monograph Series once a year (beginning 1970-71);

✔ To render reference services to all those who have bibliographical and reference questions and those who are working on M.A. theses or dissertations on Steinbeck;

✔ To issue the Annual International Steinbeck Bibliography and give it to all members free of charge;

✔ To index all worthy Steinbeckian materials, including articles, pamphlets, monographs, books, unpublished dissertations and theses, book reviews, abstracts, translations, and editions;

✔ To review books and new editions and dissertations;

✔ To exchange information on such scholarly activities as Steinbeck conferences, seminars, and lectures;

✔ To report on the research projects and trends along with works in progress;

✔ To encourage young but promising students of Steinbeck to engage in serious study of his works.

Any individual or institution with a genuine interest in John Steinbeck and his works is welcome to join the society. The member is expected to support the society in its endeavor. Since the John Steinbeck Society is a nonprofit, mutually assisting, research organization, the services and cooperation of every member are required. A member of good standing will receive the journal along with anything the society issues, free of charge. It goes without saying that unsolicited articles (at most 5-8 typed pages) are welcome as long as they are critical or expository. We do not encourage the publication of biographical ephemeras or character assassination articles and gossip, because one of our major goals is to practice serious, sensible, and meaningful criticism and evaluation of Steinbeck's works.

For the sake of those who have never heard of the *Steinbeck Quarterly* which Ball State University and the John Steinbeck Society have been publishing, I wish to introduce our editorial staff and officers who have been making this project a reality since 1968. Professor Robert DeMott, one of the guest speakers at this conference, has been serving as Associate Editor since the day the journal was initiated at Kent State University, Kent, Ohio; both Professors William V. Miller and Donald S. Siefker of Ball State are Assistant Editors; Dr. Robert L. Carmin, Dean of the College of Sciences and Humanities, is Institutional Sponsor; Drs. Dick A. Renner and Daryl Adrian are departmental co-sponsors. Furthermore, Ball State University is sponsoring the Steinbeck Monograph Series which we are launching in the 1970-1971 academic year.

Quite young as our society is, we have already accomplished a great deal. For instance, Professor Peter Lisca's article on "Steinbeck and Hemingway," which had originally been published in the *Steinbeck Quarterly* (Spring 1969), was reprinted with my permission and the author's in *Span* (December 1969), a USIA-sponsored, English-language publication in India with a circulation of 130,000. As director of the society, I answered at least 200 reference questions in 1969 by telephone and correspondence, helping a number of reference librarians at university and public and high school libraries along with individual members and M.A. and Ph.D. candidates. Professor DeMott has been contacting prominent scholars of American literature for their contributions; he has publicized our journal in important journals and newspapers at home and abroad. We are privileged to have Dr. Warren French, Chairman of the English Department, University of Missouri at Kansas City, as our president, and we enjoy his support, leadership, advice, and wisdom as we carry on our editorial duties. Furthermore, we are proud to have such prominent Steinbeckians as our active members: Professors Peter Lisca, Warren French, Joseph Fontenrose, Pascal Covici, Jr., Richard Astro, John Ditsky, Lawrence William Jones, Lester Marks, and others.

Now I would like to extend our cordial invitation to you and your university to become members. If you are interested in joining our society and in receiving the *Steinbeck Quarterly,* the Steinbeck Monograph Series, and all other publications that we issue, contact me in care of the English Department, Ball State University, Muncie, Indiana 47306.

TETSUMARO HAYASHI
Ball State University
July 17, 1970

CONTENTS

INTRODUCTION

WHEN, IN 1962, Arthur Mizener somewhat angrily referred to John Steinbeck as an "incurable amateur philosopher" whose "real but limited talent is, in his best books, watered down by tenth-rate philosophizing, and, in his worst books, is overwhelmed by it," he apparently spoke for a substantial body of critics who had finally decided to consign Steinbeck, his novels, and his Nobel Prize to the literary ash heap. Almost simultaneously, Steinbeck lost the respect of the radical sector of the literary "establishment" which found increasing evidence in his later fiction that his political matter was worn and that his depression-style militancy was hopelessly obsolete.

There were, of course, the exceptions. F. W. Watt and Warren French gave the novelist a fair if somewhat abbreviated critical examination. More importantly, Peter Lisca, whose *The Wide World of John Steinbeck* (1958) remains the definitive study of Steinbeck's fiction to date, soundly championed the novelist, stating that his work, "despite unevenness of texture, remains viable and suggests an enduring value." Then there was Tedlock and Wicker's *Steinbeck and His Critics* (1957), a collection of over two decades of selective (but often superficial) Steinbeck criticism, and Joseph Fontenrose's *John Steinbeck: An Introduction and Interpretation* (1963) which gave Steinbeck criticism a major lift by examining the novelist's perceptive use of myth and symbol through which, Fontenrose believes, Steinbeck asserts that "all life is holy, every creature

1

valuable." This notion, insists Fontenrose, accounts for Steinbeck's sentimentality, but also for his strength as a writer.

Finally, when Tetsumaro Hayashi's *John Steinbeck: A Concise Bibliography* (1967) made available to scholars the tools to examine what Warren French calls "the startling vistas, deep secret places, and rocky outcroppings" of "Steinbeck Country," the door was open for many more serious scholars to rescue the novelist from the itinerant critical voices which dismissed him as a mere journalist and deposited him in the same literary graveyard with Dalton Trumbo, James Farrell, and Tom Kromer.

The three years since the publication of Dr. Hayashi's bibliography have witnessed a resurgent interest in Steinbeck studies from a host of diverse circles. Preston Beyer, America's foremost collector of Steinbeck materials, has joined with Dr. Hayashi to form the Steinbeck Bibliographical Society (later the John Steinbeck Society of America) which, under Dr. Hayashi's editorship, publishes the *Steinbeck Quarterly* and the Steinbeck Monograph Series. In addition, Lester Marks' *Thematic Design in the Novels of John Steinbeck* (1969) represents the first attempt at a full-length thematic treatment of Steinbeck's work. Peter Lisca currently is updating his still vital book, and in May of 1969 a literary conference on *The Grapes of Wrath*, the first of its kind, was held at the University of Connecticut.

This volume of essays and the Oregon State University Steinbeck Conference at which these papers were first presented spring from this emergent interest in John Steinbeck and his work. But while it is an outgrowth of this new critical ardor, this collection differs from all earlier evaluations of Steinbeck's work. First, unlike so many conference-based works which serve only to deify a writer's work, these papers aim at frank and honest evaluations which help to measure accurately the range and magnitude of Steinbeck's achievement. Moreover, convinced that most earlier critical treatments of Steinbeck are either dated, conceived within a limited thematic spectrum, or lopsided with bias, the following articles attempt to present ten different and yet unified sides of John Steinbeck, the man, and the world about which he wrote. In search of what Steinbeck himself defined in *The Log from the Sea of Cortez* as the "toto-picture," the Oregon State Steinbeck Conference included papers from a widely disparate group of Steinbeck critics and acquaintances whose critical interpretations of Steinbeck's work and personal reflections about Steinbeck's life are as different and, at the same time as interrelated, as the world-view of the writer himself.

John Ditsky's "Faulkner Land and Steinbeck Country" is a comparative study of the way both writers use and exploit the themes of Nature in their respective works. Arguing that Faulkner deliberately created a set of man-Nature relationships (land as chronicle of human activity, as the basis for dynastic establishment, as a symbol for a covenant with man, as a link with the pagan past, and as a symbol of the "good" and "natural" influences on man), Ditsky compares Faulkner's systematic handling of Nature with what he calls Steinbeck's varied and unstructured "religion of Nature" which, he insists, goes "beyond theme and symbol" into "what must be called—if not in the usual sense—sentimentality." Analyzing nearly the entire catalogue of both writers' fiction, Ditsky demonstrates how Steinbeck's handling of Nature suffers from his inability to see "the insufficiency of treating Nature's relationships with men merely through the repetition of certain devices, rather than by developing—as Faulkner did—a set of valid prior assumptions about man and the land which his fiction might illustrate." Taking into consideration, however, Steinbeck's gradual shift of thematic focus and his insistence that he would never write the same book twice, in contrast to Faulkner who saw himself repeatedly trying to write one book successfully, Ditsky concludes that while Steinbeck may have neglected or have lost "the category and the imperative," his actual achievements may well be "the more surprising."

× Charles Shively's "John Steinbeck: From the Tide Pool to the Loyal Community" challenges the traditional notion (established almost three decades ago by Frederick Carpenter) that Steinbeck falls into a continuing skein of American philosophical thought from Emerson and Whitman to the pragmatism of William James. Instead, says Shively, Steinbeck's social philosophy more closely resembles the composite philosophical notions of the idealist philosopher, Josiah Royce. Commenting that Royce, a Californian by birth and temperament who, like Steinbeck, felt a close identity with the California landscape and its people, Shively examines Royce's Absolute Idealism which culminates in the notion of the "loyal community," the basic premise of which is that "the individualistic, self-oriented approach is not the answer," and that "the individual must change from an isolated self to an involved member of the community." Shively then compares this Roycian doctrine to the Joads' "education of the heart" in *The Grapes of Wrath*, and, supplying additional evidence from Royce's *The Philosophy of Loyalty*, argues that the basic philosophical premises of both men—the commitment to a cause and an understanding of the relationship of the individual to the whole—are nearly identical. Shively then concludes that although these parallels prove nothing conclusive about Steinbeck's knowledge of Royce, they show that the novelist "does indeed have a definite social theory" which is consistent with his conception of a unified cosmos.

In marked contrast to the comparative nature of Ditsky's essay and to the philosophical base of Shively's study, Webster Street's "John Steinbeck: A Reminiscence" is a personal and highly moving statement about Steinbeck by one of his closest friends. In the first essay of its kind on Steinbeck, Street, a long-time Monterey attorney, talks about his first meeting with Steinbeck at Stanford in 1923, and then traces various incidents which occurred during their friendship up through their last meeting in Sag Harbor in June of 1968. In addition to the many memorable reflections about Steinbeck himself, many of Street's remarks (for example, the story about the *paisanos* of *Tortilla*

Flat) help to determine the real-life base of much of Steinbeck's fiction. Perhaps, though, the most significant part of Street's commentary is his statement about the way Steinbeck learned his craft from Edith Merrilees, his short story teacher at Stanford. A landmark in Steinbeck criticism which will hopefully provide the groundwork for future studies of the novelist, Webster Street's remarks are essential to any reader or critic seriously interested in the way John Steinbeck wrote his fiction.

Returning to the scholarly vein, Robert Morsberger's "Steinbeck's Zapata: Rebel Versus Revolutionary," is a thorough and highly compelling analysis of the political and social implications of Steinbeck's neglected screenplay, *Viva Zapata!* Examining Steinbeck's handling of the screenplay's contrasting political doctrines in terms of Camus' distinction between the rebel and the revolutionary, Morsberger concludes that Steinbeck's sympathies (and those of Elia Kazan who made the movie) were with the rebel, Zapata, an agrarian reformer and "a man of individual conscience" as opposed to Fernando, the revolutionary, who "typifies the men who use the grievances of the people for their own ends, who shift and twist their course, betray any friend or principle or promise to get power and keep it." Stating further that "*Viva Zapata's* warnings against power apply equally to the extremists of left-wing revolution and right-wing reaction," Morsberger argues that "as a study of leadership and insurrection, *Zapata* has roots in *In Dubious Battle, The Grapes of Wrath,* and *The Moon Is Down*" which prove that, contrary to much critical opinion, a striking continuity existed in Steinbeck's political and intellectual concerns well after World War II.

Morsberger ends his discussion of *Viva Zapata!* by indicating that "far from being a digression into Hollywood, Steinbeck's script sums up issues that had long been central to his work. Steinbeck's continuing relevance may be seen in part by the fact that the California grape-pickers who once sang Woody Guthrie's 'Tom Joad' now display posters of Emiliano Zapata." In the next article, "In Definite Battle: Steinbeck Versus the

California Land Monopolists," social theorist James Degnan aptly shifts the focus from Zapata's rebellion against Diaz in the Mexican hills to the migrants' continuing struggle against the giant land monopolies in California's agricultural valleys. Tracing the growth of the large absentee landlords or "agri-businessmen" from Steinbeck's time until the present, Degnan levels a devastating assault against such giants as Kern County Land, DiGiorgio, and the Southern Pacific Railroad, who, during the thirty years since the publication of *The Grapes of Wrath*, have successfully evaded or turned to their own advantage every federal ordinance designed to help and protect the small land owner and itinerant farm worker. These large land corporations, Degnan insists, have made it certain that even though Tom Joad may still be around "wherever they's a fight so hungry people can eat" and "wherever they's a cop beatin' up a guy," he and his latter-day follower, Caesar Chavez, never have been able to get thirty cents for their followers when the "agri-businessman" are paying "two-bits."

While Charles Shively discusses the philosophical basis of Steinbeck's doctrine of commitment, Robert Morsberger examines one of Steinbeck's most committed heroes, and James Degnan shows the virtually insurmountable obstacles in this country against which the committed Steinbeck hero is compelled to struggle, Peter Lisca's detailed study, "Escape and Commitment: Two Poles of the Steinbeck Hero," both continues and departs from the thematic strains of the previous articles. To be sure, Lisca argues, one type of Steinbeck hero finds a deep sense of personal fulfillment in total commitment and self-sacrifice. Pointing to such characters as Jim Nolan in *In Dubious Battle* and, of course, to Tom Joad and Jim Casy in *The Grapes of Wrath*, Lisca notes that their "inspired, Christ-like, sacrificial commitment" surely qualifies them as heroic figures. At the same time, Lisca notes that there is another type of Steinbeck hero, best personified by Mack and the boys in *Cannery Row*, who, because he rejects "society's demands and escapes into individualism," rather than rejecting individualism and committing himself "to goals and values which can be realized only in society," stands at an opposite but equally heroic pole from Jim Casy and Tom Joad.

Particularly intriguing is Lisca's suggestion that one could (though Lisca does not) interpret the actions of the leading characters in *Of Mice and Men* as demonstrating either the escape or the commitment idea, or perhaps even "the nice balancing of these two themes." Carrying his analysis of these dual strains throughout most of Steinbeck's major fiction and nonfiction, Lisca notes that Steinbeck's truly heroic escapees and committed heroes appear in his writing of the thirties and forties, and he concludes that in Steinbeck's last works, his characters abandon either escape or commitment by either choosing a sense of involvement without real meaning or, more often, by simply electing to survive.

In Joel Hedgpeth's "Philosophy on Cannery Row," the center of interest appropriately shifts from Steinbeck to Ed Ricketts, whose own accomplishments as a scientist and whose heavy influence on Steinbeck Hedgpeth feels have been grossly understated. Hedgpeth, a highly competent and immovably modest maverick marine biologist in the "Rickettsian" tradition, examines the relationship between Ricketts and Steinbeck and somewhat berates the novelist for neglecting (in "About Ed Ricketts") to point out that Ricketts was a devoted scientist whose *Between Pacific Tides* (written in conjunction with Jack Calvin) is an enduring contribution to the literature of seashore biology. At the same time, Hedgpeth points to the seminal influence on Ricketts (and thus indirectly on Steinbeck) by the famed Chicago ecologist, W. C. Allee, and suggests that the Allee-Ricketts-Steinbeck relationship is fascinating and should occupy the attention of critics really desirous of understanding Steinbeck's fiction. In short, then, "Philosophy on Cannery Row" is a moving study of the relationship between Ricketts and Steinbeck which succinctly reflects Hedgpeth's belief that both men were true naturalists, devoted to achieving a synthesis of the world about them.

It is a relatively short step from Hedgpeth's "Philosophy on Cannery Row" to Robert M. Benton's "The Ecological Nature of *Cannery Row*." In this article, Benton argues that, contrary to much critical opinion, *Cannery Row* is not a minor work which suffers from a lack of structure, but is rather a tightly integrated novel which is built on a unique network of commensal relationships, the principles of which, Benton suggests, Steinbeck transferred from his extensive studies of marine organisms in the tide pools to the inhabitants and life of Cannery Row. Benton carefully points out that "not all of the relationships in *Cannery Row* are commensal," but "the fact that so many are indicates the pattern of the novel." Benton then goes on to assert that in this book Steinbeck emerges as an ecologically oriented biologist years ahead of his time who "takes the role of teacher, guiding the student to understand the relationships of organisms in an environment and to observe the processes that link organisms and place."

The next study, Charles Metzger's "Steinbeck's Mexican-Americans," opens new vistas in Steinbeck criticisms by departing from most traditional handlings of the novelist's material in that Metzger examines a given group of Steinbeck's characters on the basis of racial and ethnic distinctions. Noting that Steinbeck mentions over sixty Mexican-American characters in seven of his works, Metzger conducts an in-depth examination of a selected group of Mexican-American characters and concludes that Steinbeck—measuring them in terms of the actively operating and lofty conception of the *dignidad de la persona*—finds his Mexican-American characters interesting and admirable in that they have the ability to "merge successfully with their habitat" and because of the " 'strong but different philosophic-moral system,' which appears to make such successful merging possible for these people." Metzger then goes on to show how Steinbeck views his Mexican-American characters scientifically and romantically (but not sentimentally), and how the novelist projects through these characters "his own views of adequate human adjustment" and "an adequate life style" in which the "graceful conduct of life is the highest art."

Equally unique in its approach to Steinbeck's work is the final critical article in this volume, Robert DeMott's "Steinbeck and the Creative Process." Any similarity between these two articles ends here, however, for while Metzger is primarily concerned with theme and character, DeMott focuses on Steinbeck as a creative artist. Taking the unconventional position that at least one Steinbeck novel (*Sweet Thursday*) is better understood as "a novel of process" than as a "product novel," DeMott employs convincing evidence, particularly from *Journal of a Novel*, to suggest that *Sweet Thursday* may be a far more noteworthy novel than any of Steinbeck's critics have so far recognized. Upon reflection, it seems that the critical importance of DeMott's study may extend even beyond his arguments, for what this highly energetic and innovative scholar has done is to extend the horizon of criticism to a study of Steinbeck's craftsmanship, a facet of the novelist's work which until now has been almost totally neglected.

And so, from John Ditsky's comparison of "Faulkner Land" and "Steinbeck Country" to Robert DeMott's pioneer study of Steinbeck as a "process writer," the loosely related but uniquely integrated (in tone and dimension) collection of essays which follows suggests a new pace and a distinct change of direction in Steinbeck criticism. Neither uncritically apologetic nor pointlessly derisive, these studies rescue Steinbeck from the iron teleologies of the sentimentalist and from the disdain of the weary critic who seeks out a writer's sentimentality in order to condemn it. Taken together, these essays constitute a holistic synthesis of John Steinbeck's world view and his accomplishments as a writer. In so doing, they create at least the hope that future critics will continue to fill the gaps and relate the ostensibly unrelatable; that, as Steinbeck insists about marine biologists in the *Log*, they will "take the time to think and to look and to consider," so that "nothing is wasted, no star is lost."

One wonders whom to thank first with respect to this volume. There are, first, the highly dedicated and always helpful institutional sponsors, Dean Robert L. Carmin and my co-editor, Dr. Tetsumaro Hayashi of Ball State University, Acting President Roy A. Young, Deans Milosh Popovich, David Nicodemus, and Gordon Gilkey, and the Junior Class of Oregon State University, without whose generous and unquestioning support there would be no book at all. Special thanks must also go to Dr. Walter C. Foreman, Chairman of the Department of English at Oregon State University, to Dr. Willard Potts, Associate Professor of English at Oregon State University, and to Dr. J. Kenneth Munford and Thomas T. France of the Oregon State University Press whose advice and help in co-ordinating the Steinbeck Conference and preparing the proceedings ultimately made this volume possible. Special debts of gratitude are also reserved for my typist, Laury Dodson, who literally "lived with" the conference and the manuscripts from the beginning, and for Mike Lydall, who read proof. And finally, there is my wife, Betty, who out of unique love and understanding, has not only lived with the conference and this volume, but also with me!

RICHARD ASTRO
Oregon State University
July 1970

John Ditsky

FAULKNER LAND AND STEINBECK COUNTRY

THOUGH THE NAMES of John Steinbeck and William Faulkner might well be the first to spring to the mind of anyone contemplating a study of the relevance of Nature to character in American fiction, there are outstanding differences between the two men in the ways in which they exploit a common theme. I would suggest that though numerous parallels exist, the relatively constant employment of a regularly organized set of attitudes towards Nature as a force in fiction distinguishes Faulkner's writing from that of Steinbeck, whose varied use of such elements indicates a far-from-settled point of view.[1]

What is most surprising to the student of Nature themes in Faulkner is the discovery that there exists in his work a career-long devotion to a tightly organized and consciously applied personal "code" of beliefs, from which the single book may sometimes stray, but not the man. The basically agrarian principles of the Nobel Prize Address may be found in his earliest attempts at writing prose; and Faulkner's eventual discovery of the right means of turning those principles into fiction through the exploitation of the man-Nature relationship was a moment of conversion after which he could lapse into other interests only at the greatest peril to his artistry. For convenience and clarity, I distinguish five varieties of the use of Nature themes in Faulkner: (1) land as the chronicle of human activity; (2)

---

[1] See my unpublished doctoral dissertation "Land-Nostalgia in the Novels of Faulkner, Cather, and Steinbeck," New York University, 1967.

as the basis for dynastic establishment; (3) as the symbol for a covenant with man; (4) as a link with the pagan past and with the "dark forces" such as fertility and sexuality; and (5) as a symbol of "good" and "natural" influences on man.

Instead of Faulkner's "system," the novels of John Steinbeck show a deliberately varied series of manifestations of what may be termed a religion of Nature. Repetition of devices lends his work a certain ritualistic predictability at times, and contributes to his evident successes, but it is also to blame for much of the exaggerated intimacy between man and the land that goes beyond theme and symbol, beyond even the pathetic fallacy, into what must be called—if not in the usual sense—sentimentality. For Steinbeck the artistic struggle has been one of trying repeatedly, with varying degrees of success, for a restrained imaginative employment of his often unruly California species of the otherwise universal truths of Nature.

Faulkner's novice pieces, written in the cosmopolitan literary milieu of New Orleans, already displayed the five types of Nature usage I have described—five full years before the classic agrarian manifesto of 1930 called *I'll Take My Stand*. Quickly deciding that art ought to be "provincial,"[2] Faulkner called for a native drama that would present profoundly American themes: the vital interplay between mobile, rational men and a life-giving, timeless earth (93-97). Praising the "beauty of being of the soil like a tree" (117), Faulkner was already using the concept of a pact with the land to define men who are good, producers of life, and servants of Nature's purposes—like the Steinbeck to come. For the early Faulkner, the references are Greek and—as a bridge to the symbolist and decadent poets—Keatsian. Finding "entrails; masculinity" beneath the "spiritual beauty" of the Urn ode (117), Faulkner naturally widened his association of Nature with manhood to include human virtue

---

[2] Collected by Carvel Collins as *William Faulkner: Early Prose and Poetry* (Boston, 1962), pp. 86-89. Page numbers for this and other primary sources will be parenthetically inserted in the text after the first reference.

as well. The young Steinbeck, meanwhile, was writing college humor, and began his career as a novelist without a set of published prior assumptions.

If the apprenticeship novels of the two men are compared, the distinction becomes increasingly evident. In *Cup of Gold* (1929), Nature's use is unremarkable: pathetic fallacy, the exotic landscape of Wales, and what Merlin calls the "green monotony" of the Indies.[3] Henry progresses from the ideal Elizabeth's "flowering body" (21-24, 27) to "Mother Jungle" in Panama (124-127) in his search for the "harsh, dangerous beauty of lightning" of the Red Saint (139-141), but no defined and personal sense of Nature's literary possibilities is evident. Only as Henry approaches peace in the "immeasurable dark grotto" of "Brother Death" (196-198)—the first appearance of the cave-in-Nature motif—does Steinbeck make a tentative gesture towards authority over his materials.

Faulkner's immature writings are more extensive than Steinbeck's and begin with the *New Orleans Sketches* of 1925. The literal importance of character attitude towards the land is established in "Sunset," where a black man tragically mistakes the Mississippi Delta for the Africa of his dreams.[4] A character can be as explicitly land-related as "The Longshoreman," musing upon Nature as blood and fire (9). Greek myth and proper sexuality are identified as functions of the blood-aspect of the land, even to the point of fatality: death is part of Nature, the Franciscan "little sister" (86-91) who is sibling to Steinbeck's "Brother Death." Finally, the pastoral simplicity of David in "Out of Nazareth" shows Faulkner as interested as Steinbeck in extracting the essence of Christianity from the supposedly emasculating influence of churches.

Faulkner's first two novels show incomplete assimilation of his own prior reasoning into fictional form. *Soldiers' Pay* (1926)

---

[3] New York, 1953; pp. 17-18. I have used the most reliable current edition of Steinbeck's novels; in many cases only the Bantam paperback is in print.

[4] Carvel Collins, ed. (New York, 1968), pp. 76-85.

establishes the timelessness achieved by man in Nature,[5] an existence to which sex and death are "the front door and the back door" (295). *Mosquitoes* (1927) uses its title-insects as negative symbols, Nature's life-stealers, features of a swamp world like the dawn of time. An artist's ideal of femininity, the "virginal breastless torso of a girl,"[6] is embodied in Patricia Robyn, "sexless" yet "disturbing," though balanced by the cow-like Jenny, whose "white troubling placidity" is more fully human because more "natural" (55, 83). An artistic statement of the "dark and measured beating of the heart of things" (330), *Mosquitoes* praises those who refuse to trammel up their natural inclinations, but who seek instead a balance between intellectuality and feeling. Characters such as Januarius Jones and Talliaferro can be seen as incomplete humans in terms of their Nature-covenants, while Faulkner's saints in Nature (cow-women, idiots, madmen) may be defective as characters but are thematic idealizations of natural goodness. Still to come are such near-devils of inhumanity as Jason and Flem, who are insensitive to Nature. In between are those individuals, like Ratliff and Stevens, who can see and choose, and who try to live a rational life-with-Nature. Their predicament is the artist's; the balance they seek is precisely the one sought by Steinbeck as creator; the problem of endowing human materials with value in an amoral system.

In *Sartoris* (1929), the quest for order is defined by the contrast between the vitality of the Sartorises when the soil had full meaning for them and their tragic decline and dissipation in the landless present. Dynastic implications are actually less important to Faulkner than is often thought; I distinguish three classes of characters under this Nature-topic: (1) dynasts, who acquire land so as to establish families upon it (an initial misuse that brings eventual downfall); (2) non-dynasts, whose relationship with the land may be profound, but does not involve

---

[5] New York, 1926; p. 151.
[6] New York, 1927; p. 11.

possession for progeny's sake, or even ownership; (3) the anti-dynasts, who are oblivious to or contemptuous of the land. Without its consistent soil-referent, dynasty becomes something else for Faulkner and Steinbeck: group morality, heredity, social relationships—any of several topics which may involve blood ties without land ties.

Steinbeck's *The Pastures of Heaven* (1932) is a correspondingly ambitious attempt to deal with dynastic issues. Just as the valley of the title makes the book into a novel of sorts, two running narratives of family unify the whole: that of the Munroes, who have shaken off their own great curse only to loose "baby curses" upon the valley; and that of the Whitesides, whose grand and noble dreams are the social opposite to the Munroes' but are inextricably connected with them. In its embodiment of the Eden motif, a major step towards the themes of Steinbeck's mature works, the land dominates everyone, whether as a "curse" or as a "promise."

But though the theme of dynasty recurs throughout Steinbeck's later work, consistency in the use of it is lacking, as *To a God Unknown* (1933) illustrates. Employing the densest concentration of Nature-imagery in all of Steinbeck's fiction, *To a God Unknown* is a double example of Steinbeck's failure to learn a lesson, as he abandons a successful approach to dynastic themes in favor of an uncontrolled handling of an unfamiliar one. In its disproportion between image or symbol and plot and character as formal entities, this novel's failure evidences Steinbeck's real sort of sentimentality: excessive reliance upon Nature as force and presence to the exclusion of other agencies of realistic character motivation. Opening with a consciously Biblical scene,[7] Steinbeck plays upon the name "Valley of Our Lady": meaning not Mary, Mother of God, but Nature, Mother of Man, it is land with a "curious femaleness" to it. Joseph Wayne feels that he is going to a "wise and beautiful woman"

---

[7] New York, 1960; pp. 1-3.

(3-4), and after the land acquires more anthropomorphic qualities, the fantastic rite of sexual possession follows (7-8). Everything leading up to the scenes at the fertility altar in the woods
is a consistent excess, an indication of Steinbeck's groping towards a personal language of Nature that might work *within*
the limits of the traditional novel. Fascinating as this work is—
right up to its deliberately non-Christian tree-offering of Joseph's
son and his eventual bloodletting and rain-bringing—one cannot
get over the sheer heavy-handedness of its approach to Nature.
To a God Unknown is Steinbeck's *Mosquitoes.*⌉

But Faulkner was already at the stage of *The Sound and
the Fury* (1929) and *As I Lay Dying* (1930), major works that
sustain the developments of the apprentice pieces in all the
categories I have posited. In the former, Dilsey as patient and
enduring Negro actualizes the land's timelessness; the latter uses
such agencies as the river to objectify the backdrop against
which the Bundrens plod or scuttle.[8] Quentin's madness is aggravated by the thought that his family would "swap Benjy's
pasture" for him, a judgment of dynastic misdoing that even
Jason confirms.[9] Though Anse Bundren speaks of the need for
man to "stay put . . . like a tree" (34-35), Anse himself has never
heard what Addie calls the land's "voice" in the blood (165).
God created "sin," says Addie (166), and the acknowledgment
of the sin's naturalness is the acceptance of Nature. Quentin's
obsession with Caddy is expressed in land imagery, as is its
counterpart of Darl for Dewey Dell; both boys find sexuality
frightening, even disgusting. Addie, Dewey Dell, and Caddy—
all are one or another degree of commitment to the blood's call
and thus are literal demonstrations of what Dewey Dell signifies
to Darl by her breasts and thighs: "the horizons and valleys of
the earth" and "that caliper which measures the length and
breadth of life" (156, 97-98).

---

[8] *As I Lay Dying* (New York, 1964), p. 139.

[9] *The Sound and the Fury* (New York, 1929, 1946), pp. 217, 298.

Comparing the use of Nature in respect to character through the rest of Faulkner's major period with what Steinbeck does in his, we find the technique of *Tortilla Flat* (1935) well suited to its author's intention. Such devices as retreats to the woods, the use of wine to assist communion with and sympathy for the things of Nature, and a simplicity of character again related to the Nature-loving St. Francis develop the materials which Steinbeck's healthy irony keeps in check. *In Dubious Battle* (1936) applies these developments to the conventional novel with social problems. Dog imagery, contrasted as in Faulkner's war-produced "cattle," and the repeated use of the cave-in-Nature motif complement Steinbeck's full control of his materials. But the success of these books depends more upon the habitual attitudes of a good writer at the peak of his powers than upon the deliberate organization of a private world-view: the constitution of a Yoknapatawpha. Faulkner's *Sanctuary* (1931) expands land-as-chronicle to contrast the slow actions of men rooted in the land with the frantic haste of its despoilers. Eliot's Waste Land motif becomes for Faulkner an index to a history of wasteful action; and the horror of Temple Drake's rape with a corncob functions symbolically as well, indicating by its perversion of Nature her deprivation of naturalness. In *Light in August* (1932), the contrast between the Lena Grove and Joe Christmas parts of the book is achieved similarly: Lena's movement is slow, heedless of mile-space or clock-time; hence, artistic, even as the wagon which picks her up is "like something moving forever and without progress across an urn."[10] Christmas, violent of movement, has the "living earth against him" (367). When Hightower accepts Lena's pull to action, he is rewarded by the vision of the continuity of history which Nature, through the August light of the title, grants him (441-444, 466-467). From masterful control Faulkner passed to *Pylon* (1935), which much like *To a God Unknown* is a novel of ex-

[10] New York, 1932; pp. 4-5.

cesses, using bleak cityscape and swamp to make its point about sexuality.

Absalom, Absalom! (1936) identifies land and the past in the mind of the anguished Quentin, and the book is dominated by a figure, Sutpen, who attempts to shape the land to his own dynastic purposes instead of accepting the land's contours. But the land "tires" of Sutpen and then "destroys" him,[11] his "innocence" the price paid for his determination to carve an empire out of land which belonged to "anybody and everybody" (221). Sutpen's raw sexual vigor stands in stark relief against Rosa Coldfield's "female old flesh long embattled in virginity" (7-8), but it is failure to respect sex that partly accounts for his downfall and themes of "blood" that afflict his dynastic pretensions. At this point in Faulkner's career, the use of Nature imagery to complement characterization is fully developed and authoritative.

At the same time, two little masterpieces indicate Steinbeck's resumed control of the same materials. *Of Mice and Men* (1937) describes George and Lennie as sons of Nature seeking freedom in Nature. Characters are united by a common dream of land ownership; ironically, their disappointment is accomplished through affectionate "natural" slayings—first of a puppy, then of Curley's wife. Prefigured by a heron's killing of a snake, the death of Lennie comes after he is tormented by the vision of a giant rabbit, and the "fat of the land" credo is recited (a consistent source of irony in Steinbeck).[12] Drama in Nature also informs *The Red Pony* (1937), where Jody's initiation is assisted by the pony named after the mountains of dreaming, and whose death is a rough introduction to Nature's ways. Gitano's sense of the past turns Jody from casual animal killing to the foster-fatherhood of a new colt delivered with the help of the "half horse" Billy Buck (182). In the fourth section, the lessons

---

[11] New York, 1936; p. 12.

[12] In *The Short Novels of John Steinbeck* (New York, 1963), pp. 268-272; this volume also contains *Tortilla Flat, The Red Pony, The Moon Is Down, Cannery Row,* and *The Pearl.*

of Nature are applied to the situation of Grandfather, whose painful awareness that "westering" is over and the "race of giants" gone leads to a central statement of the American condition and its inherent disappointments, using the land on a continental scale (193-196, 198-200).

Similarly, Faulkner's *The Unvanquished* (1938) has its correlative in geography: a model of the region, a child's plaything.[13] As in *The Red Pony*, American history is encapsuled in Bayard's life: the old Sartoris code of right use of land *plus* revenge is purged of violence by the War and other events and becomes a new Sartoris code largely concerned with Nature values. And in *The Wild Palms* (1939), the sound of the palms heralds the discovery that grief is better than nothing; lacking a Mississippi setting, the title story relies upon animal imagery to reach a point of insuring futurity through reconciliation with land values. "The Old Man" is a fantastic telescoping of Genesis; its convict's real lifetime is an experience measured by the River and given value through it.

Textural similarities to *The Wild Palms* abound in that true apotheosis of Grandfather's group-man, *The Grapes of Wrath* (1939). A masterful balancing of forces, the novel is paced with running descriptions of events befalling its characters in terms of parallels in Nature. Observed changes in a dried-up landscape welcome Tom Joad home, and the stubborn turtle becomes his bestiary. The merging of Nature-religion and group-man social activism, long important in Steinbeck's thinking, occurs when Jim Casy is clearly described as a turtle-man.[14] Because the rape of the land is opposed by the love of men for one another, "Manself" begins a westward trek (204-207). Casy's self-sacrifice as Christ of Nature results in Tom's separation from his past in a ritual "coal-black cave of vines," from which he emerges with the Christian promise to return in the spirit of the people (527, 551-553, 570-572). Rewriting the Bible's flood, like Faulkner, Steinbeck has Rose of Sharon's dead child sent afloat as a

---

13 New York, 1938; pp. 3-5.
14 New York, 1939; pp. 25-26.

kind of Moses, with the mother herself auguring future strength in her famous final gesture of foster-motherhood (601-603, 609, 618-619). Yet even the achievement of a masterpiece could not confirm Steinbeck's happy arrangement of his materials, as *The Moon Is Down* (1942) illustrates simply by a change to a foreign setting.

Actually, neither man performed well when he didn't know the territory; Faulkner returned home in *The Hamlet* (1940), beginning a Snopes trilogy at every stage related to Nature. Flem Snopes is characterized by a desire to own things of Nature out of a lust after respectibility, leaving a trail of "anger" in the earth.[15] The impotent Flem's wasted field is his wife, Eula Varner, whose initial description marks the apogee of Faulkner's interest in sex (95). Ike Snopes' idyll with the cow, described as a union with cosmic history (186-189), prefigures in its reconciliation of forces Flem's eventual defeat at the hands of the Nature-related Eula and her daughter.

Corresponding to *The Hamlet* in its use of idylls in a world of animal bliss, and in its use of rampant sexuality, respectively, are *Cannery Row* (1945) and *The Wayward Bus* (1947). Indebted to the tide-pool research that gave Steinbeck his new invocation ("Our Father who art in nature . . .") (363-364), *Cannery Row* presents casual death in Nature, the sea's suggestion of death, a Doc "half Christ and half satyr" (369-371): in short, a constant recrossing of the presumed barriers between the human and animal worlds, somewhat damaged by a mixing of levels of seriousness. An idyll like the Carmel River frog hunt becomes aria to the novel's recitative. The figure of Doc, isolated by his special understanding, is a counterpart to Faulkner's Gavin Stevens. *The Wayward Bus* shows Steinbeck losing control over his set of "meanings," inserting them as philosophical decorations rather than as integral parts of his narrative. The story of the bus of fools strains to present Juan Chicoy as savior in Nature's religion: what remains of divine love after

---

[15] New York, 1940; p. 350.

Christianity's decline. Here the California landscape and its hints of sex give Steinbeck, like Faulkner, a last nostalgic fling at allegorical sexuality. *The Pearl* (1947) is more clearly allegorical and creates fewer problems. Steinbeck neatly presents the pearl in its dual aspects of precious natural growth and "gray and ulcerous" malignancy (527). Nature appears here as music, as in *Cup of Gold*.

Therefore, a decline is evident in both men as they grew mistrustful of fiction's ability to speak out unamplified. The new public Faulkner's *Intruder in the Dust* (1948) exchanges metaphor for direct rhetoric, juxtaposing the contemporary South with the drama of character; so too, in a more formally significant way, does *Requiem for a Nun* (1951), where the real interest is in the dramatic conflict of region (the interchapters) and character (the play proper). *A Fable* (1954) posits a future when there may someday be an "entire earth one unbroken machined de-mountained dis-rivered expanse of concrete paving protuberanceless by tree or bush or house. . . ."[16] Thus Faulkner is forced by historical actuality to adjust the land covenant to a concept of *continuity* with Nature, in which good men are seen as remaining faithful to the contract even when Nature's presence is unseen. Faulkner, then, consistently uses Nature to center his works, in which everything is finally about placing oneself for or against the eternal, immutable Law embodied in Nature.

Steinbeck's *Burning Bright* (1950) is, like *Requiem for a Nun,* a play in which form and language are in thrall to conception and philosophy. Joe Saul's worries about siring a son to carry on his art (his ancestors were "natural spirits") make him retreat like a "mole" into a "secret cave."[17] Mordeen's pregnancy puts her in a class with Faulkner's Lena, as her year rolls "over and over as the earth rolls" while the baby grows within her (86-90). Shifts to farm and ocean settings, however, do not

---

[16] New York, 1959; pp. 352-354.
[17] New York, 1962; pp. 14, 18, 21.

quite support the message of planned promiscuity in parenthood. *East of Eden* (1952), like *A Fable*, deals with the problem of maintaining human integrity in an age which has tossed away old values; the cave-in-Nature has become a willow tree. Overblown and yet compelling in its very sweep (again like *A Fable*), *East of Eden* ends with Lee exhorting Adam to bless Cal, remembering man's need to be "free" and *better* than "the beasts."[18] The ritualistic *"Timshel!"* closing confirms Steinbeck in a new role—rewriter of his own rewritten Bible, *To a God Unknown*. *Sweet Thursday* and *The Short Reign of Pippin IV* are late outbursts of comic spirit that parallel Faulkner's in *The Reivers*, though both are lesser works. In *Sweet Thursday*, Steinbeck nearly parodies his own use of Nature motifs; in *Pippin*, the humor is directed outward, with an easy, almost careless, use of the old imagery.

The final works are, to my thinking, immensely successful in most respects, but particularly in their swan-song virtuosity with Nature imagery. *The Reivers* (1962) is a striking, relaxed achievement in comedy, in which the narrative takes the form of a journey across land and back—a perilous cycle in which redemption is worked, initiation accomplished, and epiphany, (another birth, this time to a prostitute) sighted. Virtue is a horse race and the past is right where it belongs: in the middle of Now. The still point of the turning world in Faulkner's fiction is the point at which a character is affixed to the earth; from that point, lines of narrative stretch to infinity.

A masterful use of land imagery and a final triumph, *The Winter of Our Discontent* (1961) shifts the scene to New England, creating a Hawthornian sense of pastness in a season of conventional religious significance, Eastertide. Ethan Allen Hawley struggles with personal corruption in the form of theft and the "predator" Margie Young-Hunt,[19] assisted by the *Eden* Timshel idea here represented by good wife Mary and a daugh-

---

[18] New York, 1952; pp. 599-602.
[19] New York, 1961; p. 20.

ter who is posterity. In his "little cave" in the Hawley dock, Ethan obeys the talisman's order to go on living "else another light might go out" (308-311)—Steinbeck's final attainment of the moral stance of *The Wild Palms* and a return to the Merlin-magic of *Cup of Gold*. *The Winter* is a balanced use of Nature imagery, the achievement after which Steinbeck searched long and found only on occasion, often falling into excess, compromising forms, or losing the sense of Nature's presence. Like Faulkner, he could not do without it.

What Steinbeck suffered from, separating his work in terms of quality from Faulkner's, was partly the inability to see the insufficiency of treating Nature's relationship with men merely through the repetition of certain devices, rather than by developing—as Faulkner did—a set of valid prior assumptions about man and the land which his fiction might then illustrate. I am not praising the dynamics of uncritical pigeonholing in stressing the difference between *device* and *method*, and in emphasizing the importance of that difference to these two men. Perhaps in holding so long to the value of non-teleological thinking, Steinbeck lost both the category and the imperative. Certainly the contradictions inherent in his painful adjustment from Casy's "There ain't no sin and there ain't no virtue. There's just stuff people do" (32) to the individualistic moral code of *The Winter* aggravated the situation. Furthermore, there is the strong possibility that serious differences emerged from Steinbeck's evident desire never to write the same type of book twice, while Faulkner saw himself as trying repeatedly to get one book written successfully. Steinbeck's achievements are, in the light of these suggestions, the more surprising.

CHARLES SHIVELY

JOHN STEINBECK:
FROM THE TIDE POOL TO THE LOYAL COMMUNITY

IN 1941, with the publication of *The Sea of Cortez*, Steinbeck unveiled, for all critical eyes, the full extent of the holistic world-view which he had developed as the base for his fiction of the 1930's. This "leisurely journal of travel and research" employs ecological philosophical language to rephrase Jim Casy's fictional vision in *The Grapes of Wrath* published only two years before. As Frederick Bracher points out, the central metaphor of *The Sea of Cortez* is the tide pool.[1] The pool appears as a holistically unified cosmos which leads Steinbeck to conclude that "it seems apparent that species are only commas in a sentence. . . . And the units nestle into the whole and are inseparable from it."[2]

This publication of Steinbeck's world-view and the publication ten years later of *The Log from the Sea of Cortez*, with the addition of the section "About Ed Ricketts," has had a great effect on Steinbeck criticism. Not only do these works provide a scientific non-fictional statement of Steinbeck's doctrine of cosmic unity, but they reveal the close relationship between Steinbeck and the biologist Ed Ricketts, a relationship which had a profound impact in shaping Steinbeck's view of the cosmos. Ecology, the Pacific Biological Laboratories, Ed Ricketts all had an effect in determining Steinbeck's belief that all living things are inherently related into a Whole.

---

[1] Frederick Bracher, "Steinbeck and the Biological View of Man," *Pacific Spectator*, II (Winter 1948), pp. 14-29.

[2] John Steinbeck, *The Log from the Sea of Cortez* (New York, 1951), p. 216.

Yet, what about the actions of the individual man within this holistically unified world? The *Log* does not reveal Steinbeck's social philosophy as well as his overall world-view. For the first part of Casy's statement in *The Grapes of Wrath*, "Maybe all men got one big soul . . ." is fully explained in the *Log*; the second half, " . . . everybody's a part of"[3] and the full ramifications of the relationship of the One to the Many is not clearly stated in the *Log*. Yet Steinbeck, I contend, does have a definite social doctrine, one which fits perfectly with the holistic vision of the *Log*.

` *The Grapes of Wrath* contains the most complete expression of his social philosophy. Previous critical discussions of Steinbeck and the actions of his characters have generally dealt with these in three ways. Critics have discussed either the social philosophy only in general terms, misinterpreted it altogether, or claimed that Steinbeck had no social philosophy at all. It is my firm belief, however, that Steinbeck does have a very definite view of the individual man in relation to the unified cosmos, and he also has a somewhat systematic social philosophy.

The essay by Frederick Carpenter entitled "The Philosophical Joads" comes almost to the heart of Steinbeck's social theory but falls short at the end. Written primarily to rebut the absurd notion that Steinbeck's ideas were coming direct from Moscow, Carpenter places Steinbeck into a continuing skein of American thought from Emerson to Whitman to William James. In his haste to make a concise argument, however, Carpenter overlooks Josiah Royce, the one previous American thinker who may have influenced Steinbeck's developing social thought. The essay begins with Emerson, who provides a transcendental holistic world-view. Carpenter, however, finds that Emersonian idealism fits only to a certain point. To introduce an element of

---

[3] John Steinbeck, *The Grapes of Wrath* (New York, 1939), p. 33. All future quotations refer to this edition and will hereafter be cited by page number in the text.

social concern, Carpenter moves to Whitman and his democratic "En-Masse." From this point Carpenter claims that "the idealist becomes pragmatist" and that "in the novel a new kind of thinking takes place before our eyes."[4] The conclusion of the article states that Jim Casy "is a kind of transcendental pragmatist" (323). Carpenter has moved the democratic ideals of Whitman into action, action which Carpenter feels is analogous to the pragmatism of William James.

In the course of showing the idealistic notions as pragmatic, Carpenter states the essence of the social thought and the essence of Steinbeck's social community:

> A new social group is forging based on the word, 'en-Masse,' but here is no socialism imposed from above, here is a natural grouping of simple separate persons. By virtue of his whole-hearted participation in this new group the individual may become greater than himself . . . his strength derives from his increased sense of participation in the group.[5]

The problem with the essay is that Carpenter relies too heavily on the surface definitions of idealism and pragmatism and, because of these, chooses William James as the third thinker in the continuing skein of thought. Idealism is not all devoid of practical application. Pragmatic thinking did not suddenly burst upon the American scene with the advent of Dewey and James. In fact there is a good deal of pragmatism in Emerson's writings. An excellent example is the discipline chapter of the essay "Nature." The point here is that, while Carpenter has come close to unveiling the full extent of Steinbeck's social philosophy, in his haste to make a combination of "these mystical and poetic ideas with the realistic philosophy of pragmatism and its emphasis on effective action," (324) he mistakenly arrives at the wrong man.

Steinbeck's social philosophy does not skip from Emerson to Whitman to James; in its entirety it is consistent with the

---

[4] Frederic Carpenter, "The Philosophical Joads," *College English*, II (January 1941), 318.

[5] *Ibid.*, 319.

social thought of William James' close friend and colleague, the neglected American Absolute Idealist, Josiah Royce. An examination of *The Grapes of Wrath* and its relationship to Royce's notion of the "loyal community" can illustrate that Joseph Fontenrose's claim that "Steinbeck lacked a genuine theory of society"[6] is indeed incorrect.

Although there is no concrete evidence that Steinbeck knew of Royce or had read any of his books, their ideas concerning the individual and the community are quite analogous. Possibly Steinbeck may have come in contact with Royce's ideas and writings because of the close geographical proximity of the two men, and also their common interest in the regional aspects of California. Royce was born in Grass Valley, California, in 1855 and graduated and later taught at the Berkeley campus of the University of California, where he is officially considered a "favorite son" as a statue of him in the library testifies. Royce also was interested in the regional character of the state and in 1886 published a book entitled, *California: A Study of American Character.* Finally, it is possible that Steinbeck may have read Royce because Royce had attempted, some thirty years prior to the publication of *The Grapes of Wrath,* to deal directly with man's sense of the increasing loss of purpose and dignity of his life, a problem which was accelerated by the depression of the thirties, a problem which Steinbeck acutely felt because of his personal relationships with the migrants.

At first glance it may appear to be somewhat mistaken, if not foolish, to examine Steinbeck, whose basic philosophical premise is a naturalist's, with an idealist like Royce. This is not the case, however, for both men are primarily concerned with the same thing, the relationship of the individual to the whole. Royce, as an idealist, held that all reality is the idea, act, or experience of the mind and that there exists an "Absolute Thought" to which all other minds are related as parts to the

---

[6] Joseph Fontenrose, *John Steinbeck: An Introduction and Interpretation* (New York, 1963), p. 96.

whole. Each individual has a moral will, and each individual is a necessary part of the Absolute and makes his unique, indispensable contribution to the whole. For Royce, reality is unified into an Absolute, and man, by his moral will, participates and unites to constitute the Whole. "The One Will of the Absolute is a One that is essentially and organically composed of Many."[7] This basic precept, although of a different metaphysic, is the same as Steinbeck's naturalistic approach. In actuality, Royce's idealism and the naturalism of Steinbeck are not far removed. In terms of metaphysics, or what "ultimate reality" is, yes, there is a vast difference, but Steinbeck's approach recognized that all that "is" is really one. Reality is, in fact, a whole or an Absolute, composed and unified by the presence and actions of the individual parts to Steinbeck.

The idealism of Royce, while differing on the metaphysical question, follows along the same lines. An idealist, like Royce, is primarily concerned with the dependence of the part in relation to the whole. Idealism often has been criticized for its questioning "the genuineness of the items of experience of the world," yet this is not the true aim of the idealist, who really questions "their genuine separateness and self-sufficiency."[8] Idealism, like naturalism, is more of an approach than a strict, dogmatic interpretation of reality. The idealist is working not to prove that all reality is really an illusion, that reality exists only in the mind of an Absolute; it is not this at all. Rather, idealism starts from the belief that everything is related and then works toward an understanding of that interrelationship. The metaphysical difference between the two men is really negligible; they are, in fact, looking at the same question of the relationship of the One to the Many.

---

[7] Josiah Royce, *The Conception of God* (New York, 1897), p. 274.

[8] Clifford Barrett, *Contemporary Idealism in America* (New York, 1964), p. 16.

Warren French describes the transition that the Joads make in the novel as "a change from their jealously regarding themselves as an isolated and self-important family unit to their regarding themselves as part of a vast human family."[9] The migrants do undergo an "education of the heart," but the transition that takes place is a change from individuals to individual members of the "loyal community." The "loyal community" is best expressed by Royce in his book *The Philosophy of Loyalty* and is based upon two key definitions of the term "loyalty." Steinbeck, in writing the novel and in developing his characters, follows these definitions closely, and the result is a community which is consistent with Steinbeck's holistic views.

The basic premise for the "loyal community" is that the individualistic, self-orientated approach was not the answer. The individual must change from an isolated self to an involved member of the community. In the novel all the surviving Joads make this change, a point which is best illustrated by Tom. At the beginning of the novel Tom simply wants to "lay my dogs down one at a time." While he is roasting the rabbit for dinner, Tom rebukes all attempts by Muley and Casy to become involved in any personal conversations. Yet at the end of the novel, Tom has radically changed, "But I know now a fella ain't no good alone" (570). Tom has found that he cannot continue to wander; to survive in this new land, he needs some unifying aim. Royce, in speaking of the starting point of the "loyal community," felt that the individual is fraught with a multitude of aims and is therefore drawn toward numerous and varied approaches, urged by the driving need for some unifying principle in his life. Man as an individual is constantly vacillating from one point to another. He may seek pleasure, or power, or material possessions at one moment and then shift to a position of self-sacrifice. To Royce the problem of the "detached individual" was

> This spray of aims into which your first pure idea of a moral aim as such has been scattered, this confused and blinding cloud of

---

[9] Warren French, *John Steinbeck* (New York, 1961), p. 101.

purposes, represents for you your own moral position. Divided
in yourself, disunited, confused, you float cloud-like and inactive,
seeking unity of aim and finding none.[10]

For Royce this "unity of aim" can be achieved only by rec-
ognizing that the individual approach is no longer the way;
disillusionment and disappointment invariably will follow the
belief that one is self-sufficient. In order to achieve this unity,
man must work through the community:

Either the highest good is for humanity unattainable, or the
humanity of the future must get it in common. Therefore the
sense of the community, the power to work together, with a
clear insight into our reasons for so working, is the first need of
humanity.[11]

The belief that the individual approach is no longer valid
starts the move toward the community. As the migrants move
towards forming their community, they do so consistently with
Steinbeck's concept of man and the first definition of loyalty by
Royce. In Chapter Fourteen of *The Grapes of Wrath*, Steinbeck
sets forth his concept of man by stating that the one "quality
distinctive in the universe" is that "man will suffer and die for a
concept." This commitment to a cause forms the base of the
migrant's change from the individual "I" to the collective "We."
The migrants gradually realize that they cannot continue as isolated units but must become committed to work together. They
have committed themselves to a cause they are willing to fight
and die for; the migrants have become united in a common purpose in order to prevent disintegration, and the result is that
"the break would never come as long as fear could turn to
wrath." (592).

This commitment to a cause is the centerpoint of the "loyal
community." For Royce this "willing and practical and thor-

[10] Josiah Royce, *The Religious Aspects of Philosophy* (Boston, 1885),
p. 143.
[11] *Ibid.*, p. 175.

oughgoing devotion of a person to a cause"[12] was the first definition of loyalty. The loyalty is willing when man freely chooses
it—there must be no forced loyalties; it becomes practical because it denotes action, not merely an emotional excitement; and
it is thoroughgoing when the individual is prepared to face
hardship or death in his dedication to it. The importance of
having a community formed around one central cause or loyalty
is that

> Loyalty first unifies your plan of life, and thereby gives you what
> nothing else can give—your self as a life lived in accordance
> with a plan, your conscience as your plan interpreted for you
> through your ideal, your cause expressed as your personal pur-
> pose in living.[13]

Carpenter touched on this aspect of the Steinbeck community when he wrote that by "virtue of his wholehearted participation in this new group the individual may become greater
than himself."[14] By the end of the novel each of the Joads, from
Tom to Rosasharn, becomes committed to the cause; the "fear"
has turned to "wrath." It is a commitment which is chosen, one
that denotes action, for each of the Joads engages in some physical activity in service to the chosen cause, for which they are
willing to "suffer and die." Because of this central concept of a
chosen "loyalty," the community does not debase the individual;
rather, it unites many individual lives into the unity of one life.
By participating in this "loyal community," each migrant can
discover, as Tom, that "his little piece of soul wasn't no good
'less it was with the rest, an' was whole" (570). The community
which emerges at the end of the novel is one where each man
can find the unification of purpose. It is in this community that
Pa Joad and Uncle John find their first sense of purpose and
dignity. It is this community which unites the detached lives

---

[12] Josiah Royce, *The Philosophy of Loyalty* (New York, 1908), pp.
16-17.

[13] *Ibid.*, p. 384.

[14] Carpenter, p. 319.

in a common cause; it is of such a community that Royce spoke when he refers to how "the unity of the world is not an ocean in which we are lost, but a life which is and which needs all our lives in one."[15]

As stated earlier, both men are concerned with the relationship of the individual to the Whole. The "loyal community" is more than a grouping of people around a cause and a unification of their lives. For Royce, the spirit of this community was to become his Absolute, and it is at this point that his definition of loyalty changes. Now, Loyalty becomes the "will to manifest, so far as it is possible, the Eternal, that is the conscious and superhuman unity of life, in the form of the acts of the individual self."[16] If Steinbeck patterned his community in *The Grapes of Wrath* after Royce's "loyal community," this last definition of the term "loyalty" has profound implications. The move from the individual to the community becomes more than a simple exercise in survival; it is more than the forming of a community of devoted individuals. The community becomes the way that the individual can, by his participation in, and his devotion to, find himself in relation to the Whole. This sense of realizing oneself in relation to the Whole is a key factor for Steinbeck. He writes in the *Log* that

> . . . most of the feeling we call religious, most of the mystical outcrying which is one of the most prized and used and desired reactions of our species, is really the understanding and the attempt to say that man is related to the whole thing. . .[17]

If we carry this last concept back to the migrants' community in *The Grapes of Wrath*, the "loyal community" offers not only unity, purpose, and dignity but a place where man's "little piece of a great big soul" can be "with the rest an' was whole" (570).

Steinbeck and Royce both develop their thinking along the same lines; their world-views, anthropological and social views

---

[15] Royce, *The Philosophy of Loyalty*, p. 395.
[16] *Ibid.*, p. 357.
[17] Steinbeck, *Log*, p. 217.

aim at a unification in which man's sense of purpose and dignity can be restored. Although it cannot be conclusively proven that Steinbeck was influenced by Josiah Royce, it nevertheless remains that the community in *The Grapes of Wrath* closely resembles Royce's "loyal community." Royce's terminology and ideas concerning the individual and the community, if not the basis for Steinbeck's social philosophy, can at least illustrate that the novelist does indeed have a definite social theory; a social theory which is consistent with Steinbeck's view of a unified cosmos.

JOHN STEINBECK: A REMINISCENCE

In addressing people, I usually assume that they don't know the facts; but when the verdict comes in I often find that they know them better than I do. Well, anyway, these facts I am going to go over rather briefly concern my association with John Steinbeck from the year 1923 until the time of his death. And at the same time, since it sort of overlaps, I shall discuss my acquaintance with Ed Ricketts.

I first met John at Stanford in the spring quarter of 1923, and at that time he was living in a woodshed on San Mateo Creek. The next time I saw him was at Stanford where he was staying for a full quarter. He went to class, but I am pretty sure he did not register. The reason that he kept coming back to Stanford even though he did not have the funds to register in regular fashion was because he had so many friends on the faculty of the English department who had great hopes for him.

But before I start in on that subject, I want to mention some of the subjects that I'm not going to mention. Hence, I want to outline some of the things that are quite obvious from his writing—such as his love for the soil and what he did with it, which, with two exceptions, I am not going to dwell on at all. And then there are his political views and his humanitarianism, which obviously appear in his works, but which I will not pretend to discuss even though I know quite a bit about them from personal conversations.

We first became good friends at the English Club meetings on the Stanford campus, presided over quite often by Dr. Marg-

ery Bailey who was an authority on eighteenth-century literature, but whose love for the century was sort of telescoped from
the sixteenth century. She never gave a lecture without going
back to the germ of the Elizabethan spirit, and of course John
was very enamored with that period of literature, although one
would not know it to read his books.

I lived in Palo Alto from 1922 until 1935, and I often went
down to see John and Carol where they lived in a tiny house on
Eleventh Street in Pacific Grove that belonged to John's family.
John's father was Treasurer of Monterey County, and since the
job didn't pay a big salary and because he had three daughters
as well, he could never afford to send John to college. When I
got married in 1925, John was my best man. I have never seen
any record in any biography of Steinbeck where it even mentions the fact that he was on the west coast during 1925; he
seems to have been someplace else, but the truth is that he was
there. Then, after that, we worked together during various summers at Fallen Leaf Lodge, a resort near Lake Tahoe and now
the Stanford Alumni Summer Camp.

He and I also met quite often at what we called "the Lab."
Now I think that it would be a good idea simply to describe
this "Lab" because it was a general meeting place; for us it took
the place of the eighteenth-century coffeehouse. Moreover, we
didn't have to pay anything, so it was a real Mecca. It was a
very small room and it was occupied almost entirely by a large
bed which served as a place for people to sit. In addition, there
was a shelf for Ed Ricketts' books and a very tiny kitchen behind
that. Ed had formed Pacific Biological Laboratories in 1924. He
and a group of young scientists had gotten together and started
it. And since I'm on that subject, I might say that in 1939 John
bought quite a large block of stock in that corporation and also
loaned it a substantial sum of money which it needed very
badly.

Ed Ricketts was a very good businessman; although we
called him the mandarin because he would sit and listen to what

we were saying and would nod his head and close his eyes—he seemed to agree with everything anybody said. He was a good businessman, but not in the general sense of achieving monetary success; rather he was meticulous and very precise in everything. He had a profound influence on John, but I don't know if it had too much relation to the tide pools. What they discussed was Nietzsche, Schopenhauer, and Kantian philosophy, what's right and what's wrong, and all the other kinds of things people talk about when they're young. Ed's views on these things were largely based, I think, on Marcel Proust, at least that was the way it seemed to me at the time, and John listened very attentively because he admired Ed a great deal and had a very strong inclination toward Ed's form of scientific investigation. They would get into some kind of discussion and would go to the shelf and pick out a book, and Ed would say, "No, that's a sea rabbit," and so would pull the discussion together. We also discussed, and this was one of Ed's fetishes, I suppose, the idea that the moon had a very vital effect on what man did, not because of any mystic quality, but because it had a real gravital effect on man's bloodstream and his body. John would listen to this, and I don't know whether he agreed or not, but those were the kinds of subjects they talked about. In fact, in all the time that I listened to John and Ed discuss things, I never heard them mention political views.

We had, as a matter of fact, what might be called a non-literary association. We went to bars together—he would introduce me as Toby, "my learned friend at the bar when it's open." He would not discuss at all one of his books with me once it was written. On several occasions, he did write to me while a book was in progress, and I remember particularly his talking about *East of Eden* which he thought was the best thing he had ever done.

Actually, he was a very bad critic, and I imagine that was why he did not want to speak about his own works. He also wrote to me when he was writing *Cup of Gold*, but he didn't discuss the book very much except to say that it was sort of based on the Arthurian legend which he and another mutual friend of ours, A. Grove Day, later an English professor at the University of Hawaii, were very hep on at the time.

Before I get to something else here, I want to point out that in writing *Tortilla Flat*, John firmly believed he was writing folklore, but the truth is that his characters were real people, and proof of this can be found in the police records of Monterey. These men that he was discussing were before the police courts about once a week, particularly on Monday mornings after spending their weekends in the tank. John was careful about these characters. He knew them and saw them on the streets in various positions, usually lying down with a jug beside them, and so he checked with the man who was then Chief of Police, Monty Hellam. I think Monty filled him in on the actual activities of these people. Another man who helped John in this regard was Steve Field, a descendant of the first Chief Justice of the Supreme Court of California, and who, because his father was English and his mother was Spanish, was a real *paisano*. He told John all kinds of stories—if I had the time I could tell a lot of stories that John never wrote, but Field did give him a great deal of background.

Another person who gave him a lot of information (particularly with respect to the writing of *The Pastures of Heaven*) was Sue Gregory, a schoolteacher who had taught in a good many places in the school systems of Monterey County. She discussed things with him; *paisano* stories about the little kids in school—all their troubles and problems. The frog story in *Cannery Row* is also based on fact. Ed Ricketts had to have specimens; he had to have cats and dogs and frogs because that was his business. He would prepare these animals for histology classes and for dissection, and often these vagabonds came to his laboratory with bags full of things, mostly dead animals of one kind or another. John and I met them there a lot of times; besides, many of them lived across the street in the pipes. That was Cannery Row, and when a boiler would burn out (they are quite large and quite high) the cannery would just lay the pipes in rows right across the street from Ed's laboratory and these people would just crawl in and establish their homes.

On the academic or cultural side, I think John's short story teacher at Stanford, Edith Mirrielees, had a great deal of influence on his early writing in that she taught him to be simple and direct. Basically, she had three criteria by which a writer could evaluate his own work. First, the writer must determine whether or not he accomplished what he set out to do. Secondly, he must write a short story and not a novelette (she insisted a short story ought to be short). And finally, she believed that the story's conclusion had to be true as well as convincing.

In this regard, there is a curious thing that has always seemed to run through John's writing. This is his fondness for the spontaneous human expression, as, for instance, when somebody gets in a jam and says something and you think, "Well, that's a hell of a thing to say." In many cases, say at the end of *The Red Pony* and throughout *In Dubious Battle,* John relies on the truth of the spontaneous human reaction in speech. Critics might contend that he made up these passages, but a good many times I think he took them right from what people told him, because when you talked to John, you were conscious that he knew you a great deal better than you would ever know him.

There are a few other things I was fortunate enough to witness. Anyone who knows Steinbeck's work is, of course, familiar with the story of "The Snake." I was there when that episode took place, and I mention it to show how John had the ability to relate an incident from real life to something he created. That snake thing took place in Ed's laboratory. He had two big rattlesnakes in a cage in the lab, and he had a bunch of white rats running around. He went in and got a white rat and put it in the cage. A girl who was one of the dancers from a local vaudeville team that was passing through Monterey was there. She was just fascinated by the whole thing, but she didn't say a word. The little rat went in there, and the snake waited and pierced the rat behind the ear. The snake pulled back and the fang caught and pulled him over to one side. The rat ran around for a little while, unconscious of the fact that he was mortally wounded, and he finally died and the snake took him. That girl never said a word, and when it was over, she just got up and left and we never saw her again. Now John, I am sure, made that episode into the story of the snake and gave it sexual implications which you could not help doing if you had seen that girl.

One day we were coming back from Palo Alto on the way to Salinas and we stopped for a beer at a bar just outside Castroville. We were sitting there talking, and suddenly we heard the bartender speaking to somebody wearing bib overalls. We listened for a while. The bartender said, "And then what did you do?" and the guy went through all sorts of motions. He didn't talk with his fingers as in sign language, rather he illustrated what he did. He was mute, he could hear but could not speak. I'm certain that John based the story of "Johny Bear" on that episode. As a matter of fact, on the way back he said, "Did you pay attention to that fella, the guy in the overalls? You know he could do a lot of harm, that guy!"

In connection with *To a God Unknown,* I had been staying in Mendocino County for two vacations from college (1923-1924). I was enamored with the country because it was so green and wonderful, and I tried to persuade John to write a story about it. But he wouldn't take my word for it. I said it was like the country down by the Big Sur, but he wouldn't believe me, so we had to go and see it together. We got to Laytonville where they were having a big party and the orchestra consisted of just a piano player and a drummer who had lost his drumsticks. So John said, "That's nothing," and he went through the kitchen and took a chair (John was awfully strong) and took the rungs out and brought them back to the drummer, and the drummer went ahead with it. Then John wrote his novel.

We had all sorts of these kinds of things happen to us. The sad part of the whole business, though, is that he quit writing. I wasn't convinced of that until June of 1968 when I went back

to see him at Sag Harbor. His wife Elaine, who was very pro-
tective, heard me scolding him in the garden one day. I had
said, "John, with all the places you have been and all of the
things you know, why have you quit writing?" Elaine lit into me
and gave me "what for" for trying to get John back in the har-
ness. She knew he was ill and I didn't.

While I was there, the editor of *Life* magazine called up.
John was in the garden in one of his tool sheds, and when
Elaine told him about the call, John asked, "What does he
want?" "He wants you to go to Brussels with him," Elaine said.
"When?" "Tomorrow!" John said, "Nuts, what does he want me
to do?" "He wants you to write something for him." John said,
"Tell him when he gets back to tell me what happened and I'll
give him a hundred lines free."

I don't really know anything about literary criticism; but I
have a lot of ideas about it, and if I had the time I would probably put them in print. But coming back to this question of the
soil, I was convinced that while John was writing about the
people and places he knew, he was writing very well; but when
he left California and started to make it up, as in *Burning
Bright,* he fell apart. I talked to him once when he was out here
on the coast and told him, "John, you've never answered my
letter about coming back here; I've got a letter of yours that
asks me to try and find you about five or six acres where you
can build a house—you wanted it near the sea, not too close to
any town—what happened to all that?" John said, "I feel about
Monterey like Amy Lowell thought about Oakland." He went
on, "In the first place, the Monterey I knew isn't there any more,
the people aren't there any more; they are all different." And if
you want to know what Amy Lowell said about Oakland, she
said, "There's no *there* there."

Robert E. Morsberger

STEINBECK'S ZAPATA: REBEL VERSUS REVOLUTIONARY

In his studies of rebellion, Albert Camus makes an essential distinction between the rebel and the revolutionary. The rebel is an independent nonconformist protesting regimentation and oppression. He stands for freedom, and he is willing to die for it but reluctant to kill for it. If he backs the appeal to arms, he stops short of tyranny. The revolutionary, by contrast, speaks of liberty but establishes terror; in the name of equality and fraternity, he sets up the guillotine or the firing squad. For the sake of an abstract mankind, he finds it expedient to purge the unorthodox individual, to institutionalize terror, to enshrine dogma and dialectic.

The rebel is like Socrates, Thoreau, or Martin Luther King, whereas the revolutionary is St. Just, Robespierre, Lenin, Stalin, and the enslaving liberators of the twentieth century. Camus states that "the great event of the twentieth century was the forsaking of the values of freedom by the revolutionary movement," which contended "that we needed justice first and that we could come to freedom later on, as if slaves could ever hope to achieve justice."[1] On the other hand, "The rebel undoubtedly demands a certain degree of freedom for himself; but in no case, if he is consistent, does he demand the right to destroy the existence and the freedom of others. He humiliates no one. . . .

---

[1] Albert Camus, *Resistance, Rebellion, and Death,* trans. by Justin O'Brien (New York, 1961), pp. 90-91.

He is not only the slave against the master, but also man against the world of master and slave."[2]

This distinction runs through the work of John Steinbeck and receives its most explicit treatment in his screenplay *Viva Zapata!*, which Elia Kazan made into one of the more successful movies of 1952. Unlike Steinbeck's earlier screenplay for *Lifeboat*, this was not a collaboration; Steinbeck alone wrote both the story and the script. He worked on *Zapata* from the fall of 1948 until May of 1950 and then went on location during the filming. The finished film was very much Steinbeck's statement. The screenplay has not been published; and after the initial movie reviews, *Viva Zapata!* has been utterly neglected except for TV reruns. Peter Lisca devotes a page to it, and other Steinbeck critics do not even mention its existence. Yet it puts into final focus issues with which Steinbeck had been concerned for the previous twenty years and clarifies the relationship of issues to individuals and leaders to people. The conflict between creative dissent and intolerant militancy is extremely relevant today, and *Zapata* deserves a close analysis both as a social statement and a work of art.

As a study of leadership and insurrection, *Zapata* has roots in *In Dubious Battle, The Grapes of Wrath,* and *The Moon Is Down.* The protagonists of *In Dubious Battle* are Communists; but despite its sympathy for the strikers, the novel is profoundly critical of revolutionist tactics. Steinbeck commented that, "Communists will hate it and the other side will too."[3] The battle is indeed dubious, for the means do not justify the end. Mac, the Communist organizer, is the professional and ruthless revolutionary to whom people are merely tools of guerrilla warfare. Zapata is given leadership by the already aroused people, but Mac is the manipulator who instigates a strike that he knows

---

[2] Albert Camus, *The Rebel,* trans. by Anthony Bower (New York, 1957), p. 284.

[3] Peter Lisca, "John Steinbeck: A Literary Biography," *Steinbeck and His Critics,* eds. E. W. Tedlock, Jr. and C. V. Wicker (Albuquerque, 1957), p. 10.

will lose but that is part of "the long view" towards a brave new world. For the cause, it does not matter which individuals suffer. To win the workers' confidence, Mac risks the life of a woman in labor. He exploits the death of friends, for "We got to use whatever material comes to us."[4] He hopes some of the strikers will be killed, for "If they knock off some of the tramps we have a public funeral; and after that, we get some real action"; and when he is told that innocent men may be shot, he replies, "In a war a general knows he's going to lose men."[5] Mac advises Jim Nolan, the Communist novice, "Don't you go liking people, Jim. We can't waste time liking people."[6]

Thus for the determined revolutionary, issues are more important than individuals. Jim Nolan is human enough at first, but he develops into such a True Believer that his "cold thought to fight madness" scares even Mac. When Mac smashes the face of a high school boy, Jim says, "he's not a kid, he's an example . . . a danger to the cause," and beating him "was an operation, that's all."[7] Even Mac now feels that Jim is not human, but Jim insists that "Sympathy is as bad as fear."[8] Like Ethan Brand, he has lost his hold on humanity and justifies torture in the name of human brotherhood.

Mac and Jim rarely discuss dialectic; they seem motivated less by party dogma than by a need for the transfiguring experience of revolution that Doc Burton calls "pure religious ecstasy."[9] The two Communists awaiting martyrdom in "Raid" have a similar emotion; but as Camus notes, "Politics is not religion, or if it is, then it is nothing but the Inquisition."[10]

---

[4] John Steinbeck, *In Dubious Battle* (Modern Library edition, New York, n.d.), p. 60.

[5] *Ibid.*, p. 335.

[6] *Ibid.*, p. 115.

[7] *Ibid.*, p. 274.

[8] *Ibid.*

[9] *Ibid.*, p. 254.

[10] Camus, *The Rebel*, p. 302.

In reaction to *In Dubious Battle* and *The Grapes of Wrath,* some right-wing critics of the time denounced Steinbeck as a revolutionary, even as a Communist. It is no longer necessary to refute these charges; Steinbeck was never a Communist except in Mr. Hines' sense that "A red is any son-of-a-bitch that wants thirty cents an hour when we're payin' twenty-five."[11] In Russia, critics noted that *The Grapes of Wrath* did not follow the orthodox line, but B. Balasov said the book has a "definite revolutionary direction."[12] Actually, as Chester E. Eisinger and others have pointed out, Steinbeck's migratory farm workers have their roots in Jeffersonian agrarianism. Far from wanting state collectivization, they long, like Lennie and George, for a place of their own. Steinbeck was an ardent advocate of private property and wrote in *The Grapes of Wrath,* "If a man owns a little property, that property is him . . . and some way he's bigger because he owns it."[13]

Steinbeck predicted that if revolution should come, it would not be the work of professional agitators but would be an overflow of outrage in response to organized oppression. Under conditions of farm labor in California, "the dignity of the man is attacked. No trust is accorded them. They are surrounded as though it were suspected that they would break into revolt at any moment. It would seem that a surer method of forcing them to revolt could not be devised."[14] Steinbeck's solution was punishment of vigilante terrorism and encouragement for the agricultural workers to organize within a democratic framework.[15] Camus notes that "a change of regulations concerning property without a corresponding change of government is not a revolu-

---

[11] John Steinbeck, *The Grapes of Wrath* (Viking edition, New York, 1939), p. 407. All other quotations in this paper from Steinbeck's published works are from the Viking editions except Footnotes 4-9, 14-15, 17, 30, 35.

[12] James W. Tuttleton, "Steinbeck in Russia: The Rhetoric of Praise and Blame," *Modern Fiction Studies,* XI (Spring 1965), 80.

[13] Steinbeck, *The Grapes of Wrath,* p. 50.

[14] John Steinbeck, *Their Blood Is Strong* (San Francisco, 1938), p. 13.

[15] *Ibid.,* p. 29.

tion but a reform,"[16] and this is what Steinbeck supported. But unless the change came quickly, he predicted that "from pain, hunger, and despair the whole mass of labor will revolt."[17]

Such a spontaneous uprising of the people occurs in *Viva Zapata!* Emiliano Zapata is not a conscious revolutionary but a natural leader of a justifiably rebellious peasantry. In the film, he first appears as a member of a delegation to the dictator Diaz. Like the dispossessed Okies of *The Grapes of Wrath*, the farmers complain that an anonymous "they" have taken the village land. The delegates claim ownership since before history and reinforced by papers from the Spanish crown and the Mexican republic. The question of ownership is recurrent and critical to Steinbeck. In *The Grapes of Wrath* and *Their Blood Is Strong*, he urges not collectivization but a fair redistribution of land among private holders. Later in *Viva Zapata!* when Don Nacio, a landowner sympathetic to the peasants, entertains some large planters, he defends the Indian villagers' right to their land and urges the planters to "Give the land back. You don't need it. You have so much. . . . We're all in danger. If we don't give a little—we'll lose it all."[18] Don Garcia replies indignantly that he paid for the land and therefore owns it, but Don Nacio insists that the Indians lived there for a thousand years, "since before the Conquest," and that such living makes them the true owners.[19] His attitude and that of the peasants is like the tenant men in *The Grapes of Wrath* who say, ". . . it's our land. We measured it and broke it up. We were born on it, and we got killed on it, died on it. Even if it's no good, it's still ours. That's what makes it ours—being born on it, working it, dying on it. That makes ownership, not a paper with numbers on it."[20]

Zapata's role is that of agrarian reformer, not a revolution-

[16] Camus, *The Rebel*, p. 106.

[17] Steinbeck, *Their Blood Is Strong*, p. 30.

[18] John Steinbeck, *Viva Zapata!*, unpublished screenplay, shooting script final, May 16, 1951, 20th Century-Fox, p. 45. All quotations are used by permission of 20th Century-Fox.

[19] *Ibid.*, pp. 45-46.

[20] Steinbeck, *The Grapes of Wrath*, p. 45.

ary remolder of society. When Diaz questions the delegation's ownership of the land, Zapata emerges as spokesman for the group. He speaks common sense and farmers' folkways, not dialectic, and tells Diaz that corn, not the courts, is essential to the farmers. When Diaz advises the men to check the boundaries but refuses them official permission to cross armed and guarded fences to do so, Zapata replies that they will take his advice. We then see a close-up of Diaz' hand circling Zapata's name on the list of delegates.

Though he is more articulate than the others and takes more initiative, Zapata does not seek leadership; circumstances and the people thrust it upon him. Steinbeck shows the revolution beginning like Concord and Lexington; the embattled farmers trying to survey their lands are attacked by rurales, who begin machine-gunning them. Zapata, who is mounted, lassoes the machine gun and enables most of the farmers to escape. Here and in later episodes, he has no plans but rather an impetuous reaction to tyrannic violence. But as the Mayor in *The Moon Is Down* tells Alex Morden, who hit and killed a Nazi overseer, "Your private anger was the beginning of a public anger."[21] Likewise Casy and Tom Joad at first have only a spontaneous and improvised response to episodes of outrage, but gradually they learn to make long-range plans.

Zapata meanwhile hides in the hills with a handful of followers. There he is sought out by Fernando Aguirre, who first appears as a young man with a typewriter, which he calls "the sword of the mind." Zapata at this point is still illiterate; he is no intellectual but is in tune with the ways of people and the land. One of the more moving scenes in the film is his urgent plea on his wedding night that his wife teach him to read. It is significant that he speaks Aztec as well as Spanish; this enables him both to get information from the peasants and to hear and empathize with their sufferings. Unlike this man of the people, Fernando has no background that we ever discover; we gradually learn that he is the revolutionary who will betray anyone

---

[21] John Steinbeck, *The Moon Is Down* (New York, 1942), p. 96.

for his own ends. At this point Fernando is an emissary from Madero, "the leader of the fight against Diaz." Before agreeing to become an ally, Zapata sends Pablo to Texas to look in Madero's face and report what he sees; Zapata wants to evaluate a man, not an ideology.

While Pablo is away, Zapata receives a pardon and is hired to appraise horses for his wealthy patron, Don Nacio. He begins courting the wealthy, aristocratic Josefa Espejo. He has a private life to lead and a promising future. But again, indignation intervenes. Camus notes that "rebellion does not arise only, and necessarily, among the oppressed, but . . . it can also be caused by the mere spectacle of oppression of which some one else is the victim. In such cases there is a feeling of identification with another individual."[22] Steinbeck composes such a scene very carefully. We first see eggs being beaten for rubbing down Arabian stallions. A hungry little girl dips her finger into the mixture and licks it. The mother, seeing Zapata observe this, slaps the child, who looks away in shame, and Zapata also looks away in shame. The manager says such people are lazy and orders servants to rub down the horses better. When the manager beats a starving boy whom he catches stealing food from the horses, Zapata can no longer stand by; he risks his job and his pardon by knocking the man down. Zapata's employer asks, "Are you responsible for everybody? You can't be the conscience of the whole world," but Zapata can only answer, "He was hungry."[23] Yet Zapata does not want involvement; he longs for privacy, and so he apologizes to the manager. At this strategic moment, Pablo returns from Madero, accompanied by Fernando, who offers Zapata a command. Zapata's response is that he does not want to be a leader: "I don't want to be the conscience of the world. I don't want to be the conscience of anybody."[24]

---

[22] Camus, *The Rebel*, p. 16.
[23] Steinbeck, *Viva Zapata!*, p. 28.
[24] *Ibid.*, p. 33.

Yet he cannot be passive in the face of oppression. So when he encounters rurales dragging a prisoner by a noose, Zapata cuts the man loose and thus becomes an outlaw a second time. This man (significantly named Innocente) had crawled through a fence at night to plant a little corn. Again, Zapata has no plan but improvises in reaction to events. Fernando, the revolutionary, has plans, however, which do not object to the sacrifice of the individual, so Fernando smiles when Zapata rides off an outlaw. Zapata can serve the cause, and his private misfortune may be public good.

Camus observes that "when a movement of rebellion begins, suffering is seen as a collective experience"; the rebel "identifies himself with a natural community."[25] Likewise, Steinbeck notes in *Sea of Cortez:* "Non-teleological notion: that the people we call leaders are simply those who, at the given moment, are moving in the direction behind which will be found the greatest weight, and which represents a future mass movement."[26] This is what now happens to Zapata. When rurales capture him, the people accompany him in an increasingly massive procession until it is so large that it stops the column. The mere presence of this silent, spontaneous procession forces the captain to free the prisoner. The people bring Zapata's white horse and by this gesture make him their leader. Before, he had no followers, only a handful of friends. Now he takes command. Fernando urges him to cut the telegraph wires. "Captain: 'Don't touch that! This is rebellion!' " In a fine dramatic pause, Zapata looks at his brother Eufemio, whose machete is raised; then he orders, "Cut it."[27]

The film has been building symbolically to this moment. First, Zapata has overseen the cutting of the boundary wire. Next, he has cut the noose around Innocente's neck—but too late; the soldiers have dragged the man to his death, and Zapata

---

[25] Camus, *The Rebel,* pp. 22, 16.
[26] John Steinbeck, *Sea of Cortez,* in collaboration with Edward F. Ricketts (New York, 1941), p. 138.
[27] Steinbeck, *Viva Zapata!,* p. 44.

concludes that he should have cut the rope first and then talked. After that, we see Zapata himself pulled by a halter. Thus, cutting the wire becomes a symbolic culmination, severing the bonds of oppression and signifying decisive action.

The film now presents a number of quick scenes of guerrilla warfare culminating in Diaz' defeat. Zapata says thankfully, "The fighting is over."[28] This campaign has been like the first or real Russian revolution, and fully half of the script deals with it. But instead of bringing peace and reform, the revolution is spoiled by the professionals, who inaugurate a series of betrayals. In a dramatically symbolic scene, Steinbeck shows Zapata first torn between the conflicting claims of power and the people. As the victorious Zapatistas are celebrating, Fernando arrives with a document from Madero designating Zapata "General of the Armies of the South." Brother Eufemio hands him a general's ornaments, while an Indian woman gratefully gives him "a dirty bouquet of live trussed chickens"; the last shot shows him standing with the chickens in one hand and the ornaments in the other. It is significant that Fernando is the emissary for power. Reveling in victory, the celebrants all get drunk except Fernando, who remains cold sober.

> EUFEMIO: I know what's the matter with you. You are unhappy because the fighting is over.
> FERNANDO: Half victories! All this celebrating and nothing really won!
> EUFEMIO (*embracing him*): I love you—but I don't like you. I've never really liked you.
> FERNANDO: There will have to be a lot more bloodshed.
> EUFEMIO (*losing patience with him*): All right! There *will* be! But not tonight! (*gives him bottle*) Here—enjoy yourself! Be human![29]

It is never clear what Fernando wants or why he thinks there must be bloodshed, but he is intolerant of anything less

---

28 *Ibid.*, p. 63.
29 *Ibid.*, p. 66.

than absolutism. He resembles Jim Nolan when the latter declares, "I'm stronger than you, Mac. I'm stronger than anything in the world, because I'm going in a straight line. You and all the rest have to think of women and tobacco and liquor and keeping warm and fed."[30]

Madero is now in charge. He is presented as a good man, mild and well-meaning but bewildered. When Zapata presses him for immediate land reform, Madero insists that rebuilding must take time and be done carefully under the law. Zapata is impatient, though willing to give Madero a chance, but Fernando condemns the President as an enemy.

PABLO: But you're his emissary, his officer, his friend . . .
FERNANDO: I'm a friend to no one—and to nothing except logic
. . . This is the time for killing.[31]

He apparently wants a purge, and with some reason, for as the delegation departs, Huerta and a group of fellow generals enter and dominate Madero. Huerta advises him to shoot Zapata now, but Madero insists that he does not shoot his own people and that Zapata is an honest man. With true revolutionary logic, Huerta replies, "What has that got to do with it??!! A man can be honest and completely wrong!"[32] From here on, Zapata's inevitable death is foreshadowed, and the film takes a tragic turn.

While the guerrillas are disarming under Madero's orders, Huerta and the regular army pull a coup and march against Morelos. Madero has been like Kerensky, insisting on a constitutional government; now the ruthless professional revolutionaries take over. Madero falls into Huerta's hands and is murdered. The Zapatists resume their guerrilla warfare against the new oppressor. Again Zapata is victorious; but in the process, power inevitably involves him in evil. Camus asks "whether innocence, the moment it becomes involved in action, can avoid

---

[30] Steinbeck, *In Dubious Battle*, p. 274.
[31] Steinbeck, *Viva Zapata!*, p. 71.
[32] *Ibid.*, p. 74.

committing murder."[33] Zapata's forces are ambushed, and among the suspected traitors is Pablo, accused of meeting with Madero after Huerta betrayed the revolution. Pablo's defense is an eloquent plea for peace. Madero, he says, was trying to hold Huerta in check.

> He was a good man, Emiliano. He wanted to build houses and plant fields. And he was right. If we could begin to build—even while the killing goes on. If we could plant while we destroy . . .

Fernando interrupts harshly, "You deserted our cause!"

> PABLO: Our cause was land—not a thought, but corn-planted earth to feed the families. And Liberty—not a word, but a man sitting safely in front of his house in the evening. And Peace, not a dream—but a time of rest and kindness. The question beats in my head, Emiliano. Can a good thing come from a bad act? Can peace come from so much killing? Can kindness finally come from so much violence (he now looks directly into Emiliano's immobile eyes). And can a man whose thoughts are born in anger and hatred, can such a man lead to peace? And govern in peace?[34]

This point becomes the focus of the rest of the film, and it is an issue that concerned Steinbeck for a long time. Doc Burton, his spokesman in *In Dubious Battle*, tells Jim, "in my little experience the end is never very different in its nature from the means. Damn it, Jim, you can only build a violent thing with violence." When Jim insists, "All great things have violent beginnings," Doc replies, "We fight ourselves and we can only win by killing every man."[35]

Eventually, Fernando helps to kill Zapata; but meanwhile his inflexible logic requires the death of Pablo, even though it was Fernando who first brought Pablo and Madero together. Now he tries to make even Zapata his tool. While Zapata himself is executing Pablo at the latter's request, a courier arrives and Fernando informs him, "General Zapata is busy." We hear

---

[33] Camus, *The Rebel*, p. 4.
[34] Steinbeck, *Viva Zapata!*, pp. 88-89.
[35] Steinbeck, *In Dubious Battle*, pp. 253-254.

the shot that kills Pablo; and Fernando then says, "General Zapata will see you now."[36] Only once before had Emiliano been called "General Zapata," and that too was by Fernando. Otherwise, he had been simply a campesino, always approachable, as when a young boy, who like Zapata had lassoed a machine gun, demanded Zapata's white horse when offered a reward. Zapata's giving the horse to him foreshadows his renouncing power and returning it to the people. Now, setting up formal audiences and executive isolation, Fernando has become a barrier between Zapata and the people.

When some of the people turn against him, Zapata realizes that Pablo was right. Pablo, in his patience and wisdom, resembles Anselmo in *For Whom the Bell Tolls;* his friend the Soldadera, a Pilar-type woman warrior, tries to kill Zapata with Pablo's knife. The guards urge her death, but Zapata lets her go, insisting, "The killing must stop! Pablo said it. That's all I know how to do!"[37] Whenever he has been tempted to act the tyrant, one of the people has reminded him of reality.

Zapata's refusal to take anything for himself leads to his death. Huerta is beaten, and Fernando and Villa propose Zapata for President. Though he refuses office, Zapata does take command in Mexico City, while Carranza and Obregon replace Huerta as the military opposition. An Old General proposes that Zapata form an alliance with these commanders "for the good of Mexico." Intervening, Fernando violently refuses, insisting, "The principle of successful rule is always the same. There can be no opposition. Of course, our ends are different."[38] He advises Zapata to kill the General; yet when Zapata relinquishes power, it is Fernando who joins Carranza and Obregon and gives the Old General the plan that betrays Zapata to his death.

Again, it is a reminder from the people that recalls Zapata from power. A delegation from Morelos calls upon him to com-

---

[36] Steinbeck, *Viva Zapata!,* p. 90.
[37] *Ibid.,* p. 94.
[38] *Ibid.,* p. 101.

Zapata

Ed Ricketts

Photograph of Emiliano Zapata courtesy of Twentieth-Century Fox. Photographs of Ed Ricketts and the Ricketts-Steinbeck letter, courtesy of Stanford University Press.

plain that his brother Eufemio has been taking their lands and women. Zapata at first equivocates, asks for time, then (in a re-enacting of the first audience with Diaz) circles the name of the spokesman for the group. Suddenly, with horror, he realizes what he is doing and what he is about to become. He rejoins his people, saying, "I'm going home. There are some things I forgot."

> Fernando: So you're throwing it away. . . . I promise you you won't live long. . . . In the name of all *we* fought for, don't leave here!
> Emiliano: In the name of all *I* fought for, I'm going. [italics mine]
> Fernando: Thousands of men have died to give you power and you're throwing it away.
> Emiliano: I'm taking it back where it belongs; to thousands of men.

When Fernando refuses to go with him, Zapata says, "Now I know you. No wife, no woman, no home, no field. You do not gamble, drink, no friends, no love. . . . You only destroy. . . . I guess that's your love."[39]

In this context Zapata's love story is significant. The courtship and marriage of Zapata and Josefa (the only treatment of romantic love Steinbeck had so far attempted) is historically inaccurate but artistically valid. The real Zapata had dozens of women and numerous bastards. The screen Zapata is more saintly, but the love story humanizes him, adds a tragic dimension, and also enables Steinbeck to include some humor and folklore. In a picaresque episode, Zapata and Eufemio first approach Josefa and her duenna in church; the outlaw proposes while she is praying. Her father has predicted that Zapata's wife will become a peasant, and she rejects her suitor with the words, "I have no intention of ending up washing clothes in a ditch and patting tortillas like an Indian."[40] Later, Zapata courts

---

[39] *Ibid.*, p. 106.
[40] *Ibid.*, p. 21.

her more formally in a humorous scene with traditionally stilted proverbs; the tiger is momentarily tamed. The drama of their wedding night, when she starts teaching him to read while crowds celebrate outside, is moving; they are like earnest and innocent children with the book between them. Josefa does not appear again until near the end, when we see her washing in a stream with Indian women. "Her father's prediction has come true—she is practically indistinguishable from the others."[41] But she is ennobled, not debased, by the change. Though she appears in only five comparatively brief scenes, the part is memorable, with humor, humanity, and pathos. The script conveys a sense of their whole life together, and her anguish on the eve of the fatal ambush is the climax of Zapata's sacrifice.

Once home, Zapata initiates a program of planting and building along with the fighting against Carranza and Obregon, and tells the people:

> About leaders. You've looked for leaders. For strong men without faults. There aren't any. There are only men like yourselves. . . . There's no leader but yourselves.[42]

Thus when Fernando accomplishes Zapata's betrayal and murder, the people can go on.

In *The Moon Is Down*, the Nazi conquerors insist that Mayor Orden think for his people and keep them in order. Orden replies that his people "don't like to have others think for them" and that "authority is in the town," not in any individual.[43] Corell, the quisling traitor, tells the Nazis, "When we have killed the leaders, the rebellion will be broken."[44] This issue had long been of concern to Steinbeck. Considering Steinbeck's self-reliant reformers, Frederic I. Carpenter asked in 1941, "What if this self-reliance lead to death? What if the individual

---

[41] *Ibid.*, p. 115.
[42] *Ibid.*, p. 109.
[43] Steinbeck, *The Moon Is Down*, pp. 36, 41.
[44] *Ibid.*, p. 171.

is killed before the social group is saved?"[45] Though the Nazis do order the Mayor's death, Dr. Winter observes, "They think that just because they have only one leader and one head, we are all like that . . . but we are a free people; we have as many heads as we have people, and in a time of need leaders pop up among us like mushrooms."[46]

Zapata's wife, fearing a trap, asks, "If anything happens to you, what would become of these people? What would they have left?" His answer is, "Themselves."

> JOSEFA: With all the fighting and the death, what has changed?
> EMILIANO: They've changed. That is how things really change— slowly—through people. They don't need me any more.
> JOSEFA: They have to be led.
> EMILIANO: But by each other. A strong man makes a weak people. Strong people don't need a strong man.[47]

A passage from *The Grapes of Wrath* anticipates the ending of *Zapata*. When Tom Joad leaves to become a rebel against oppression, Ma tells him, "They might kill ya."

> Tom laughed uneasily. "Well, maybe like Casy says, a fella ain't got a soul of his own but on'y a piece of a big one— an' then—"
> "Then what, Tom?"
> "Then it don' matter. Then I'll be aroun' in the dark. I'll be ever'where—wherever you look."[48]

Perhaps the people don't need a leader, but they need a legend. When Zapata is shot to ribbons from ambush, some of the peasants emerge. The Soldadera, who had tried to kill Zapata, now composes his body, for his death is an atonement that makes him again one of her people. Lazaro, an old veteran who knew Zapata well, examines the body and spurns it, saying that such a shot-up corpse could be anybody. "I fought with

---

[45] Frederic I. Carpenter, "The Philosophical Joads," *College English*, II (January 1941), 325.

[46] Steinbeck, *The Moon Is Down*, p. 175.

[47] Steinbeck, *Viva Zapata!*, p. 121.

[48] Steinbeck, *The Grapes of Wrath*, p. 572.

him all these years. Do they think they can fool me? They can't
kill him . . .

> YOUNG MAN: They'll never get him. Can you capture a river?
> Can you kill the wind?
> LAZARO: No! He's not a river and he's not the wind! He's a man
> —and they still can't kill him! . . . He's in the mountains.
> You couldn't find him now. But if we ever need him again
> —he'll be back.[49]

As they look up to the mountains, they see Zapata's white horse,
which escaped and is now walking towards the peak.

At first this may seem like a conventional Hollywood ending, but in fact it is historically and artistically appropriate. If
Lazaro's name recalls Lazarus and thus links Zapata with
Christ, there is a Mexican context for resurrection as well in the
Montezuma myth that makes the slain emperor into a once and
future king. Many of the people of Morelos did indeed refuse to
believe that Zapata was dead; some insisted the corpse was not
his, and others claimed to have seen his horse galloping into the
southern mountains. In actuality, Zapata was not alone but
accompanied by a bodyguard when he was killed, and his horse
was not white but roan. The white horse comes from Diego
Rivera's mural of Zapata. Thus slight distortions of fact may
come closer to the ultimate meaning of Zapata's death.

Some movie reviewers faulted the film for simplifying or
distorting history, but the simplification is a virtue here. Steinbeck cuts through the complexities of campaigns and the incredible intricacies of political intrigues to get at what he sees
as the essence of the events. The latter is what most bothered
some reviewers. The movie had a mixed reception, praise going
to the action sequences and to performances by Anthony Quinn
(who won an Academy Award) as Eufemio, Joseph Wiseman as
Fernando, and Harold Gordon as Madero, with divided opinion
on the effectiveness of Jean Peters as Josefa and Marlon Brando

---

[49] Steinbeck, *Viva Zapata!*, pp. 127-128.

Permanent

Pacific Biological Laboratories

Pacific Grove, California

February 15, 1948

TPH
Here 'tis

Stanford University Press
Stanford University, Calif.

Gentleman:

May we withdraw certain selected parts of "Between Pacific Tides" which with the passing years badly need revision? Science advances but Stanford Press does not.

There is the problem also of the impending New Ice Age.

Sometime in the near future we should like to place our order for one (1) copy of the forthcoming (1948, no doubt) publication,

"The Internal Combustion Engine, Will it Work?"

Tell them that's Science too!

Sincerely,

John Steinbeck

Ed Ricketts

P.S. Good Luck with
"A Brief Anatomy of the Turtle"

Ed Ricketts

as Zapata. *Newsweek's* reviewer called the film a "sincere trib-
ute" with "a careful and intelligent characterization," *The
Christian Century* found it "brilliant," *Commonweal* termed it
"a thoughtful film," and the Chief of the American History
Division of the New York Public Library praised it as "exciting
and impressive."[50] But *Holiday* complained of a "tedious and
oratorical screenplay by John Steinbeck," *Life* lamented Steinbeck's "mouthfuls of political platitudes," *The New Yorker*
found the film entertaining aside from "Mr. Steinbeck's murky
views on revolution," and *The New Republic* objected to
"squelchy aphorisms of a kind we have had before from the
Oakies [sic] of California and the doomed heroes of the Nor-
wegian underground."[51]

Actually, resemblances to *The Grapes of Wrath* and *The
Moon Is Down* reveal a continuity in Steinbeck's intellectual
concerns, no more reprehensible than the reappearance of central themes in the work of Hawthorne and Henry James. A
study of *Zapata* can enrich one's appreciation of the earlier
books. The aphorisms occur in an appropriate context of action, and they by no means constitute the greater part of the
script. When Hollis Alpert complained of so-called "stock
phrases" like "A strong people does not need a strong man,"
Laura Z. Hobson asked Steinbeck about them, and he replied,
"I interviewed every living person I could find in Mexico who
had known or fought with Zapata. Again and again I heard
those words or their first cousins." Against charges of bombast
and cliché, he said, "Whenever a man disagrees with the ideas

----

[50] *Newsweek*, XXXIV (February 4, 1952), 78; *The Christian Cen-
tury*, LXIX (April 23, 1952), 510; Philip T. Hartung, *Commonweal*, LV
(February 29, 1952), 517; Gerold D. McDonald, *Library Journal*,
LXXVII (February 15, 1952), 311.

[51] *Holiday*, XI (May 1952), 105; *Life*, XXXII (February 25, 1952),
61; John McCarten, "Wool from the West," *The New Yorker*, XXVII
(February 16, 1952), 106; *The New Republic*, CXXVI (February 25,
1952), 21.

involved in a book, a play, or a movie, and cannot publicly admit his disagreement, he attacks on ground of grammar or technique."[52]

Elia Kazan explained some of the political pressures brought against the film. Noting that the Mexican revolution had other leaders besides Zapata, he claimed that he and Steinbeck were particularly fascinated by Zapata's renunciation of power in the moment of victory. "We felt this act of renunciation was the high point of our story and the key to Zapata himself." When they submitted the script for the opinion of some prominent Mexican film makers, these men "attacked with sarcastic fury our emphasis on his refusal to take power." Kazan claims that he and Steinbeck felt such criticism came from the Mexican Communists, who wanted "to capitalize on the people's reverence for Zapata by working his figure into their propaganda. . . . Nearly two years later our guess was confirmed by a rabid attack on the picture in *The Daily Worker,* which parallels everything the two Mexicans argued, and which all but implies that John invented Zapata's renunciation of power. No Communist, no totalitarian, ever refused power. By showing that Zapata did this, we spoiled a poster figure that the Communists have been at some pains to create."[53] Curiously, some liberals then accused Steinbeck and Kazan of McCarthyism, while at the same time the far right denounced them for dealing with Zapata at all, since all rebels must be Communists. Kazan again replied that, "There was, of course, no such thing as a Communist Party at the time and place where Zapata fought. . . . But there is such a thing as a Communist mentality. We created a figure of this complexion in Fernando," who "typifies the men who use the just grievances of the people for their own ends, who shift and twist their course, betray any friend or

---

[52] Laura Z. Hobson, "Trade Winds," *The Saturday Review,* XXXV (March 1, 1952), 6.

[53] Elia Kazan, "Letters to the Editor," *The Saturday Review,* XXXV (April 5, 1952), 22.

principle or promise to get power and keep it." Here, then, is Camus' revolutionary, by contrast to Zapata the rebel, whom Kazan calls "a man of individual conscience."[54]

The controversy continued with a criticism of the film by Carleton Beals, an expert on Mexico and one-time instructor to Carranza, who claimed that Zapata's abdication of power was pure fiction. Kazan again replied, defending Steinbeck's extensive research, which turned up numerous conflicting accounts of Zapata's mysterious departure from Mexico City. "John had to make choices and he made them with an eye to implementing his interpretation."[55]

Steinbeck, then, was not so much reconstructing history as using it to convey ideas. Likewise, Camus says of *The Rebel* that his book attempts to "present certain historical data and a working hypothesis. This hypothesis is not the only one possible; moreover, it is far from explaining everything. But it partly explains the direction in which our times are heading."[56]

Steinbeck's interpretation seems to have been reinforced by his recent visit to Russia; the same year that he began his screenplay, he published *A Russian Journal*. In it he repeatedly condemned the concept of the strong man, objecting to the humorless museum mementos of Lenin and the ubiquitous iconography of Stalin. He recalled that he and photographer Robert Capa "tried to explain our fear of dictatorship, our fear of leaders with too much power, so that our government is designed to keep anyone from getting too much power, or, having got it, from keeping it."[57] By contrast to the official Soviet "heroes of the world," Steinbeck admired the "little people who had been attacked and who had defended themselves successfully."[58]

---

[54] *Ibid.*

[55] Elia Kazan, "Letters to the Editor," *The Saturday Review*, XXXV (May 24, 1952), 25, 28.

[56] Camus, *The Rebel*, p. 11.

[57] John Steinbeck, *A Russian Journal* (New York, 1948), p. 57.

[58] *Ibid.*, pp. 134-135.

The true rebel need not be a warrior at all except against prejudice, ignorance, and conformity. An earlier Steinbeck screenplay, *The Forgotten Village,* also set in Mexico, presents such a rebel in the person of Juan Diego. This story deals with the conflict between superstition and science in a mountain village. The well water has become contaminated, and children are dying. The villagers rely on a conjure woman for cures; but Juan Diego, a teen-age boy, together with the schoolteacher, learns that bacteria cause the sickness. When he tries to persuade his people to get medical aid and vaccinations, they denounce him and say it is better for the children to die and go to heaven than for them to seek the help of science. Juan Diego goes alone to the city to get medical help for his village. En route, he meets a soldier who asks him why he travels. When Juan Diego explains, the soldier replies,

> You will think I who am a soldier should like to fight. I am an old soldier. I was a boy from a village like you before I was a soldier. Yours is the true people's work . . . saving, not killing; growing, not dying.[59]

Here is the alternative to Fernando, to whom Zapata's last words are, "You only destroy."

When Juan Diego returns with help, the *curandera* strikes him, the village denounces him, and the father drives him away. Thus the rebel suffers for his individuality. Juan Diego departs with the doctors and takes up the study of science and medicine. "And the change will come, is coming; the long climb out of darkness. . . . as surely as there are thousands of Juan Diegos in the villages of Mexico," the doctor predicts. The last line of the screenplay affirms the independence and integrity of the rebel: "And the boy said, 'I am Juan Diego!' "[60]

The final rebel is the artist, in this case Steinbeck himself, who noted in *A Russian Journal* that "although Stalin may say that the writer is the architect of the soul, in America the writer

---

[59] John Steinbeck, *The Forgotten Village* (New York, 1941), p. 99.
[60] *Ibid.,* p. 143.

is not considered the architect of anything. . . . In nothing is
the difference between the Americans and the Soviets so marked
as in the attitude, not only toward writers, but of writers toward
their system. For in the Soviet Union the writer's job is to encourage, to celebrate, to explain, and in every way to carry
forward the Soviet system. Whereas in America, and in England, a good writer is the watch-dog of society. His job is to
satirize its silliness, to attack its injustices, to stigmatize its
faults. And this is the reason that in America neither society nor
government is very fond of writers."[61]

Viva Zapata!'s warnings against power apply equally to the
extremists of left-wing revolution and right-wing reaction. The
film not only interprets the past but foreshadows events that
have since occurred. Philip T. Hartung judged that, "Few historical movies have stated so well the post-revolutionary problem or asked so disturbingly the questions that must be answered about all new leaders."[62] Far from being a digression
into Hollywood, Steinbeck's script sums up issues that had long
been central to his work. Steinbeck's continuing relevance may
be seen in part by the fact that the California grape pickers who
once sang Woody Guthrie's "Tom Joad" now display posters of
Emiliano Zapata.

[61] Steinbeck, *A Russian Journal*, p. 164.
[62] Philip T. Hartung, *Commonweal*, LV (February 29, 1952), 517.

JAMES P. DEGNAN

IN DEFINITE BATTLE:
STEINBECK AND CALIFORNIA'S LAND MONOPOLISTS

CONTRARY TO ITS TITLE there is nothing dubious about the major battle of Steinbeck's *In Dubious Battle;* for the battle in this novel is as clear, as definite, as the major battle in *The Grapes of Wrath*. It is the age-old battle between California's land monopolists and California's small family farmers and farm workers; the battle between genuine farmers who live on and work the land and land speculators, absentee landlords (or, as they prefer to call themselves these days, agribusinessmen); the battle between a plantation system and a homestead system; the battle between a fascist state and a democratic state.

In fiction such as the above, Steinbeck dramatizes the fact that the common enemy of the migrant farm worker and of the small family farmer has always been the huge landowners, the land monopolists of whom, Mac, a central character in *In Dubious Battle*, rightly says: "They control everything, land, courts, banks. They can cut off loans, and they can railroad a man to jail, and they can always bribe plenty."

In Steinbeck's fiction (as in fact), it is not the small family farmer—the farmer who needs only a few workers at harvest time and who works side by side with those workers—who exploits the migrant workers; it is the huge landowner, often the absentee landlord, who exploits both. In *The Grapes of Wrath*, for example, a small farmer who wants to pay the Joads more money explains why he can't: "The Farmers Association sets the price," he says, and "do you know who runs the Farmers Association? The Bank of the West. That bank owns most of this valley, and it's got paper on everything it don't own." A member from the bank, the small farmer tells the Joads, has recently called on him and warned him that if he dares pay his workers more, the Bank of the West (undoubtedly Steinbeck's name for the Bank of America) will not give him a loan on his next year's crop.

In the unusual event the small farmer or migrant worker does not bend to economic intimidation, we know from Steinbeck's fiction, that the landowners, hiding behind the phony front of the Farmers Associations, turn to violence. Screaming "communist," they form vigilante committees or simply turn loose the company-owned police: They beat and jail and murder the migrants; and they burn the homes and barns and crops of the disobedient small farmers.

The fact of Steinbeck's fiction, the fact of the fascistic control of California agriculture by a handful of huge landowners, is documented in many historical and sociological texts. It is, for instance, documented in various of the writings of Henry George, the great champion of the single tax; in James Bryce's classic *The American Commonwealth;* and in Carey McWilliams *Factories in the Fields*—the non-fiction counterpart of *The Grapes of Wrath.*

Those texts and others like them demonstrate that California—unlike the American Midwest and East and like the American Deep South—developed, not as a democratic system of homesteads, of family farms, but as an autocratic system of plantations, a system dominated by a handful of land monopolists determined to hold the land, determined to keep the small farmer from owning land. " . . . ever'thing in California is owned," the Okie returning to Oklahoma warns the Joads. "They ain't nothin' left. An' them people that owns it is gonna hang on to it if they got ta kill ever body in the world to do it." Texts like *Factories in the Fields* demonstrate that the statement of Steinbeck's Okie is not entirely an exaggeration.

Further, such texts document the fact well known to most students of American history that California's most powerful land monopolists—individuals who have always prided themselves on being champions of law and order—illegally acquired and sustained their land empires. These texts show, for example, that many, if not most, of California's biggest land monopolies were created—to mention only a few of the illegal means—from fraudulent Mexican Land Grants; from fraudulent claims against the Desert Land Act of 1876; and from criminal collusion between California land grabbers and officials of the federal government. These texts tell the story of the illegal creation of such land empires as Kern County Land, Southern Pacific Railroad (a story dramatized in Frank Norris' *The Octopus*), and the Irvine Corporation, to name a few of California's oldest, most powerful, and most corrupt land monopolies. And, finally, these texts tell in fact the story Steinbeck tells in fiction: the story of the ruthless and systematic exploitation of the migrant worker by the land monopolists—a story that is as old as the state of California.

I don't wish to belabor the facts presented so ably by these texts; rather, I wish to bring them up to date. I wish to show that the not so dubious battle between Steinbeck's characters and California's land monopolists continues today. Further, I wish to show that it is not only the small farmer and the migrant laborer in California who are the victims of the land monopolies Steinbeck deplores, but every American taxpayer.

"If I recognized that union of farm workers," said the owner of a small grape ranch in Delano, California, "I'd be without a loan on next year's crop." A statement from Steinbeck's fiction? A statement from the 1930's? Not at all. The above is the answer to a question I asked in the fall of 1965—when, on assignment for *The Nation,* I was doing a piece on Cesar Chavez and the grape strike in California's Joaquin Valley. Having explained that he, like many other small growers, did not oppose the union—that, indeed, since he was already paying his migrant helpers more than the union was asking, he was *for* the union—the small grower went on to say that it was the big growers, the big landowners in the Valley, owners like the DiGiorgio Corporation and Schenley Industries, who opposed the union. Explaining that because his farm was relatively small, that because he lived on his land and worked it himself, he needed only a few workers and that paying them decent wages wasn't really much of a problem, he declared that it was the big growers—many of them absentee landlords—the growers who needed literally thousands of seasonal workers, who stood to reap enormous profits by keeping wages depressed and the labor market flooded, which is to say, by keeping the union out. For these owners, he explained, keeping the union out was as financially advantageous as it had been to keep the bracero program in.

But, to repeat, although the small grower was for the union, he did not dare publicly support it. For, should he have done so, he would have incurred the wrath of the huge landowners in the Valley and would have, by his testimony, ended up with no loan on his next year's crop.

How can a small farmer of the 1960's be intimidated in the same way as his counterpart in the 1930's, for example, the small farmer in Steinbeck's fiction? Examine the relationship between California's land monopolists—landowners like DiGiorgio—and the rest of California's power structure—the banks and utilities, for instance—and you can easily find the answer. DiGiorgio, in 1965 the biggest distributor of grapes and tree fruits in the world, and the Bank of America, an institution that in 1965 financed almost 60 percent of California's agricultural production, shared at that time (as they still do) no fewer than four directors, a relationship one economist has called "rare even in the world of higher capitalism."

Besides the interlocking directorate with Bank of America, DiGiorgio shared then (as now) directorates with, to mention only a few, such powerful organizations as Pacific Gas and Electric, Pacific Telephone and Telegraph, Bank of California, and the Union Oil Company.

The same is true of the other major California land monopolists. Kern County Land, for example, shares directors with, among others, California Packing Corporation (Del Monte Products), Crocker Citizens Bank, Bank of California, Wells Fargo Bank, Pacific Gas and Electric, and Pacific Telephone and Telegraph.

And not only do the land monopolists control the banks and utility companies so vital to the survival of the small farmer, they control the very market on which the small farmer must sell his product. DiGiorgio, for example, controlled 93 percent of the Met Food Corporation in 1965, which, in simple terms means that if the small grape grower mentioned above wanted an Eastern—e.g., a New York City—market for his table grapes, he was forced to play along with DiGiorgio.

It is not, however, only the small farmer and the migrant farm worker who are the victims of California's land monopolists; it is the American taxpayer. Just as the taxpayer was the main financier of the outrageous bracero program—a program which, by importing foreign labor chiefly for the benefit of the big landowners, kept Americans out of work and on welfare—so, also it is the taxpayer who has been and who continues to be the main financier of the vast empires of the land monopolists.

How? By providing the monopolists with hundreds of millions of dollars worth of federally financed water—water which does not legally belong to the monopolists. This giveaway of the public's water has been called by Senators Wayne Morse and Paul Douglas "a scandal rivaling Teapot Dome . . . with water rather than oil involved." What the Senators are talking about, in general, is the violation of the reclamation law that has taken place on most of California's federal reclamation projects—e.g., in the Imperial Valley, in Southern California, and in the Sacramento Valley—and, specifically, the violation of that law on the San Luis (Westlands) unit of the Central Valley Project in the San Joaquin Valley. What is happening on this project is representative of what has happened on most of the other federal water projects in California: the United States Department of the Interior is pouring away over a half-billion dollars of the American taxpayer's money to irrigate an area in which nearly 80 percent of the land, according to reclamation law, is ineligible to receive water.

The main purpose of the Reclamation Law of 1902, largely a creation of President Theodore Roosevelt, was to prevent the few from monopolizing the land and from amassing huge speculative profits and attendant political powers at the expense of the many, i.e., of the taxpayers who finance federal reclamation projects. (One has only to read Steinbeck to see how thoroughly President Roosevelt's law has been frustrated.) Therefore, the law contains a strong anti-monopoly, anti-speculation provision (the 160-acre limitation) which forbids delivery of federally subsidized water to lands in excess of 160 acres unless the owners of those acres agree by written contract to sell those acres within ten years at a price *not inflated by the availability of federally subsidized water*—in other words, at dry land values.

Now considering that desert lands worth $5 an acre have often skyrocketed to $1,000 and more an acre on the mere promise of federal irrigation waters, it isn't difficult to understand that dry land values were (and are) very reasonable indeed, prices within the means of the family farmers for whom they were intended and that (1) the law guaranteed a continuing land pool for such farmers and (2) guaranteed the taxpayer that his dollar would go to subsidize real farmers, not land speculators.

Designed to encourage the democratic system of family farms developed in the Midwest under the Homestead Act and to prevent the development in the Far West of the plantation system, designed to prevent land monopolies and huge speculative profits for the few at the expense of the many, the federal reclamation projects have usually had just the opposite effect. Presently, for example, on the Westlands project in the San Joaquin Valley, the federal government, by illegally delivering water to land monopolists—water conservatively estimated to be worth $1,000 an acre as an outright subsidy—is perpetuating rather than preventing or breaking up land monopolies, such monopolies, for example, as Kern County Land, DiGiorgio Corporation, Standard Oil Corporation, Southern Pacific Railroad, J. G. Boswell Company, and the Tejon Ranch (the latter property owned by the *Los Angeles Times* publisher, Norman Chandler). Southern Pacific Railroad, which presently owns in California over 3.5 million acres of land, owns 150,000 acres on the Westlands project alone. Thus, besides incalculable speculative enrichment of its holdings as potential urban property, on this project Southern Pacific stands to gain $150 million as an outright gift of the American taxpayers.

If the Secretary of the Interior doesn't enforce the law, it won't be enforced; and that no Interior Secretary since Harold Ickes has dared conscientiously enforce the law is testimony to the tremendous political influence of California's land monopolies. Despite their political power, though, the monopolists have always feared that another Ickes might someday appear, and they have made many efforts (1) to have the law abolished or (2) to have it, in their words, "realistically revised." Their efforts to have Congress abolish the law, however, have always failed. Faced with the issue, Congress has always voted to support what the U. S. Supreme Court declared in 1958: that the 160-acre limitation should be upheld because it is the taxpayers' only guarantee that "great public expenditures will not go in disproportionate share to a few but will be used for the greatest good of the greatest number."

The monopolists' argument for having the law "realistically revised" is that the law, to quote the monopolists, is "medieval and outmoded"; a law designed for the farm situation of 1902, not for today when only the huge corporate farm is "efficient" enough to meet our local and national agricultural needs. And the sad thing is that the public, including many urban liberals who should know better, has largely allowed itself to be hoodwinked into believing this.

First, even though it is *not* the issue, the family farm is not inherently less efficient than the corporate farm. Reports like the excellent Sasuly report from UCLA indicate the contrary.

If the family farmer got a fraction of the subsidies the government heaps on the huge agri-industrialists, Sasuly contends, if he did not have to fight the vertical integration of the big corporation farms, if he were guaranteed a market for his products, the family farmer might well be considerably more efficient than the corporate farmer. But, to repeat, efficiency is not the issue. Arguing over the relative efficiency or inefficiency of family versus corporate farms is merely a smoke screen laid down by the monopolists to conceal the real issue. Which issue is quite simple: When the land monopolists argue that the 160-acre limitation isn't realistic, when they say it is "outmoded" and needs substantial "revision," they are really saying, as history has proved time and again, that they want no limitation placed on them. Southern Pacific, for example, has publicly declared that it has no intention of breaking up its 150,000-acre empire in the San Joaquin; does Southern Pacific expect us to believe that it must have 150,000 acres in order to farm efficiently? What the monopolists are really saying is that they want both their land monopolies and their unearned speculative profits *plus* a continuation of the subsidized water that will perpetuate their monopolies and profits. Make no mistake, when monopolists like Southern Pacific oppose the 160-acre limitation, it is clear that they are not speaking as farmers—big, little, or middle sized, efficient or not efficient—they are speaking as out-and-out land speculators.

While it is obvious that neither federal nor state officials today are going to enforce the law in California—Ronald Reagan, for example, wants the law abolished—enforcement of the law has suddenly become an issue with California's conservationists. Led by groups like the Sierra Club, the state's conservationists have just awakened to the fact that the Reclamation Law of 1902, rather than being "medieval and outmoded," is actually a farsighted conservation law—a law that anticipates the major problems of land and water use in California today; and the conservationists may be the catalyst for its enforcement.

Since World War II California has been, to quote the popular title, "Going, Going. . . ." Precious open space, forests, streams, mountains, irreplaceable agricultural lands—all these are going under asphalt and concrete, factories and freeways, shopping centers and housing tracts, with incredible speed. And the main reason, of course, is unchecked land speculation. Most of the natural resources that have been destroyed have been in private hands—hands greedy for the quick profits urbanization brings. In some areas of California such speculators are difficult, indeed, impossible to control legally; but this is not the case in the vast regions covered by reclamation law. In these regions today there are nearly one million acres held in violation of the excess lands provision of reclamation law— 400,000 of them in the area of the Westlands project alone. There is no better way to guarantee that these acres remain as open space or as agriculture, no better way to conserve these lands and to protect their resources for the future, no better way to prevent their being converted into urban sprawl, than for the government, exercising its rights under reclamation law, to purchase these lands at dry land values.

Such purchase would not only guarantee conservation of these lands, but it would enable the government, acting in the interest of the taxpayer, to do such things as lease the land to real farmers; to fight rural poverty by leasing land to farmers driven off their farms into the already hopelessly overcrowded cities; and to use the revenues from these lands to replenish the U. S. Treasury and to provide grants to education.

Further, such purchase is really the taxpayers' only hope for being protected against the land monopolists using federal water to create, not only agricultural empires, but urban empires. This is what the giant Irvine Corporation, by evading reclamation law, has done in Southern California. Naively believing that Irvine would keep its lands in agriculture, the federal government poured federal waters from the Colorado River to Irvine, waters that made the Irvine land valuable, not only as agriculture, but as potential urban property; and, of course, when it was profitable, Irvine urbanized its agricultural lands. Thus, millions of federal dollars, not only in water but in crop subsidies, dollars intended to guarantee America a continuing agricultural product, went, literally, down the drain.

And today the same thing is happening in the San Joaquin Valley. Two things were necessary here for commercial development: (1) water and (2) the freeway. Interstate 5 opened up the west side of the Valley for development, and the federal government, apparently believing the land here will remain for agricultural use, continues to provide the water, courtesy of the American taxpayers. San Joaquin land monopolists like Di-Giorgio are already moving out of agriculture. Last year, Di-Giorgio entirely ceased grape production and moved into the real estate business on its grape farms, putting these farms up for sale—in direct violation of reclamation law—not only at prices only speculators could afford, but worse, actually advertising the land for its speculative value. And unless reclamation law is enforced it is not difficult to imagine other San Joaquin land monopolists—e.g., Southern Pacific, J. G. Boswell (to whom the federal government last year alone paid over $4 million in cotton subsidies), Standard Oil, and Kern County Land—doing very much the same thing.

The battle of groups like today's conservationists against California's land monopolists is a continuation of the battle Steinbeck dramatized in his fiction; hopefully, it is a battle that eventually will be won by those whom Steinbeck would wish victorious.

Peter Lisca

ESCAPE AND COMMITMENT:
TWO POLES OF THE STEINBECK HERO

In one of the little essays Steinbeck did for the *Saturday Review* in 1955, "Some thoughts on Juvenile Delinquency," he writes as follows concerning the relationship of the individual to the society in which he lives: " . . . I believe that man is a double thing—a group animal and at the same time an individual. And it occurs to me that he cannot successfully be the second until he has fulfilled the first." The nice organic relationship which Steinbeck here postulates near the end of his writing career is seldom to be met in his fiction. Much more frequently we are presented with characters who choose one of two extremes—either to reject society's demands and escape into individualism, or to reject individualism and commit themselves to goals and values which can be realized only in terms of society.

In Steinbeck's very first novel, *Cup of Gold* (1929), in the figure of Merlin, is found not only an extreme example of escapism, but one of its most eloquent philosophers. As a young man, a greatly talented bard, he had taken up a hermit's life in a stone tower on a lonely mountain top. There he has grown old with his harp and his books of history and mythology, a legendary figure in his own lifetime. It is suggested that the cause of this self-imposed isolation may have been his losing a bardic contest through political influence. The consequent disillusionment is reflected in his remarks to the young Henry Morgan, who has come to consult him before going off into the world to make his fortune: " 'I think I understand,' he said softly. 'You are a little boy. You want the moon to drink from as a golden cup; and so, it is very likely that you will become a great man—

if only you remain a little child. All the world's great have been little boys who wanted the moon; running and climbing, they sometimes caught a firefly. But if one grows to a man's mind, that mind must see that it cannot have the moon and would not want it if it could—and so it catches no fireflies." Merlin goes a step further, and adds as a compensation for this loss of worldly ambition the attainment of community with mankind ("He has the whole world with him . . . a bridge of contact with his own people. . . ."), whereas the worldly successful and therefore immature man "is doubly alone; he only can realize his true failure, can realize his meanness and fears and evasions."

The fascination which this general intellectual posture had for the early Steinbeck is evident from another character in the same novel. James Flower is from an aristocratic, well-educated English family who in despair at his harebrained impracticality buy him a plantation in the Barbadoes, where he cannot embarrass them. "And so he had grown wistfully old, on the island. His library was the finest in the Indies, and, as far as information went, he was the most learned man anywhere about. But his learning formed no design of the whole. . . . His mind was a sad mass of unrelated facts and theories. In his brain, as on his shelves, Caesar's Commentaries stood shoulder to shoulder with Democritus and a treatise on spontaneous generation." In Steinbeck's first novel, then, we have two variations on the theme of escape; and although neither is the main character, Henry Morgan's life ultimately suggests that they were both wiser.

In Steinbeck's next book, *The Pastures of Heaven*, three years later, we find James Flower's same impracticality and indiscriminate bookishness in the character of Junius Maltby, who is treated at greater length and with more obvious sympathy. Again he is a man of "cultured family and good education." Also, his way into an escape from a worldly existence is an enforced one, a threat to his health, but is clearly congenial to him. Through his abstraction and impracticality the little farm which comes to him by marriage becomes unproductive; his wife's two children by former marriage die of influenza because they are undernourished while Maltby helplessly reads aloud *Treasure Island* and *Travels With a Donkey*. Finally his wife dies in childbirth, leaving him a son whom he names Robert Louis. Maltby makes an attempt at practicality by hiring an old German to work the farm, but within a week the two men become boon companions and spend their days sitting around together "discussing things which interested and puzzled them —how color comes to flowers—whether there is a symbology in nature—where Atlantis lay—how the Incas buried their dead. In the spring they planted potatoes, always too late, and without a covering of ashes to keep the bugs out. They sowed beans and corn and peas, watched them for a time and then forgot them. The weeds covered everything from sight." The three of them manage to survive, barefoot, ragged, ill-fed, but happy in their discussions of the battle of Trafalgar, the frieze on the Parthenon, the Spartan virtues, Carthaginian warfare, and other erudite topics. Steinbeck's description of their conversation reflects its impracticality in terms of their agricultural theories: "They didn't make conversation; rather they let a seedling of thought sprout by itself, and then watched with wonder while it sent out branching limbs. They were surprised at the strange fruit their conversation bore, for they didn't direct their thinking, nor trellis nor trim it the way so many people do."

Surprisingly, the boy Robbie thrives in this environment and becomes a natural leader at school, fascinating fellow pupils and teachers alike with his poise and exotic knowledge. The school board, however, is more interested in Robbie's ragged clothes. Although the story ends with Maltby and his son on their way to San Francisco and a return to a clerkship in order to provide the material benefits of society, it is interesting that in a separate publication of this story, three years later, Steinbeck adds an epilogue: "I've often wondered whether Junius got a job and whether he kept it. . . . I for one should find it difficult to believe he could go under. I think rather he might have broken away again. For all I know he may have come back

. . ." There follows an imaginary reconstruction of their return, concluding with the words, "I don't know that this is true. I only hope to God it is."

Clearly, then, in his first two books of fiction Steinbeck demonstrates a serious interest and sympathy for what in today's slang might be called the "drop-out." A case might be made for discussing here his next novel, *To a God Unknown,* published just a year after *The Pastures of Heaven,* for in that novel too we have a character who in a secluded valley pursues a way of life unsanctioned by his society, in this case a dedication to mysticism and fertility rituals. In that novel, too, we find a hermit who, again in modern parlance, "does his own thing" with no Society For the Prevention of Cruelty to Animals nearby. But these similarities are peripheral, and not central to the theme of escape versus commitment. A more direct relationship can be established with the novel that followed in two years— *Tortilla Flat.*

This novel introduces two important changes in Steinbeck's treatment of the "drop-out" (which is a better term than "escapee"). First, whereas the earlier characters of this type had deliberately rejected the clear advantages available to them, in the form of family and education, these Mexican-American *paisanos* find themselves initially in a poor position to compete in modern society. Second, and more important, the "drop-out" is no longer a shy, retiring, solitary, but an active, gregarious member of a whole community of "drop-outs." They have in common with their prototypes in earlier novels, however, a disinclination toward industrious labor and a disrespect for material property, for through the loss of possessions comes sorrow— "It is much better never to have had them." They also share a love of the contemplative life. True, sometimes pure contemplation arrives at the practical result of procuring a jug of wine or a chicken in a highly imaginative manner, but the process is enjoyed as much as the result, and sometimes consoles them for material lack or loss. The morning after Danny's other house burns down, for example:

. . . Danny came out on his porch to sit in the sunshine and to muse warmly of certain happenings. He slipped off his shoes and wriggled his toes on the sunwarmed boards of the porch. He had walked down earlier in the morning and viewed the square black ashes and twisted plumbing which had been his other house. He had indulged in a little conventional anger against careless friends, had mourned for a moment over that transitory quality of earthly property which made spiritual property so much more valuable. He had thought over the ruin of his status as a man with a house to rent; and, all this clutter of necessary and decent emotion having been satisfied and swept away, he had finally slipped into his true emotion, one of relief that at least one of his burdens was removed.

At other times their contemplation, although expended on subjects less impressive than the Parthenon or the burial rites of the Incas, is equally leisured and undirected:

In the morning when the sun was up clear of the pine trees, when the blue bay rippled and sparkled below them, they arose slowly and thoughtfully from their beds.

It is a time of quiet joy, the sunny morning. When the glittery dew is on the mallow weeds, each leaf holds a jewel which is beautiful if not valuable. This is no time for hurry or for bustle. Thoughts are slow and deep and golden in the morning.

Pablo and Pilon in their blue jeans and blue shirts walked in comradeship into the gulch behind the house, and after a time they returned to sit in the sun on the front porch, to listen to the fish horns on the streets of Monterey, to discuss in wandering, sleepy tones the doings of Tortilla Flat; for there are a thousand climaxes on Tortilla Flat for every day the world wheels through.

They were at peace there on the porch. Only their toes wriggled on the warm boards when the flies landed on them.

Other mornings begin similarly, and one evening the solitary contemplation of Pilon leads to a moment of mystic revelation and Franciscan prayer. "He raised his face into the sky and his soul arose out of him into the sun's afterglow. . . . Pilon went up to the sea gulls where they bathed on sensitive wings in the evening. . . . 'Our Father is in the evening,' he thought. 'These birds are flying across the forehead of the Father. Dear birds, dear sea gulls, how I love you all. . . . Dear birds, . . . fly to our Lady of Sweet Sorrows with my open heart.' And then he said the loveliest words he knew, 'Ave Maria, gratia plena—'"

Perhaps these examples create a suspicion that what is described here is not really the contemplative life but the lazy one. For Steinbeck, the distinction was not clear-cut. In Sea of Cortez (1941), he writes: "Only in laziness can one achieve a state of contemplation which is a balancing of values, a weighing of oneself against the world and the world against itself. A busy man cannot find time for such balancing." And laziness has other virtues as well: "We do not think a lazy man can commit murders, nor great thefts, nor lead a mob. . . . And a nation of lazy contemplative men would be incapable of fighting a war unless their very laziness were attacked. Wars are the activities of busy-ness."

In his fiction up to 1935, then, stretching over six years of the Great Depression, beginning with minor characters and culminating in Tortilla Flat with a whole community of "dropouts," Steinbeck demonstrates a serious and sympathetic interest in the theme of escape from society. And only in one short story published in 1934 does he recognize even the existence of contemporary social issues. Instead, he set his fiction in the seventeenth, late nineteenth, and early twentieth centuries, thus in a sense performing as author the same escape as his characters.

All of this changes in 1936 with the publication of In Dubious Battle, which remains the best strike novel in the English language. Here Steinbeck demonstrates not only his detailed, quite professional knowledge of communist labor organization tactics in the field, but also presents us with central characters who are totally committed to bringing about substantial changes in American society. Prior to the strike novel, only "The Raid" had suggested this involvement by Steinbeck and had projected such commitment in the characters. In light of the importance which Judeo-Christian symbols and reference have in The Grapes of Wrath, it is interesting that this first treatment of proletarian subject matter should also find such references necessary. There is the master-apostle relationship of the two organizers, the portrait of their anonymous precursor who inspires them by his example, their own sense of sacrifice for mankind, and certain allusions in the dialogue. Root tells the vigilantes, "We're all brothers," and "It's all for you. We're doing it for you. All of it. You don't know what you're doing." Later, in the hospital, Dick, the more experienced organizer, repeats his instruction to the neophyte: "It wasn't them. It was the System. You don't want to hate them. They don't know no better" (which is the Christian concept of hating the sin and not the sinner). And the neophyte recalls that in the Bible ". . . it says something like 'Forgive them because they don't know what they're doing.'" The importance of these references is that they underscore the sacrificial nature of the action. The organizers had warning of the vigilantes' approach and could have escaped, but chose to stay. They were determined that what had been written by their precursor should be brought to pass—"The men of little spirit must have an example of steadfastness. The people at large must have an example of injustice."

This commitment and self-sacrifice is even more extreme in Jim Nolan of *In Dubious Battle,* and in them he finds his personal fulfillment. "I used to be lonely," he says, "and I'm not any more. If I go out now it won't matter. The thing won't stop. I'm just a little part of it. It will grow and grow." This commitment is accompanied by an even wider Christian reference. Whereas the neophype in the short story had been merely *willing* to be used as "an example of injustice," Jim Nolan of the strike novel is so anxious as to have a martyr complex. Over and over he tells Mac, his mentor, "I want to get into it" and "I want you to use me." Only after he has gotten into it and has been wounded is he happy and sure of how strongly he is committed: "'Then I got hurt. . . . I got to know my power. I'm stronger than you, Mac. I'm stronger than anything in the world, because I'm going in a straight line. You and all the rest have to think of women and tobacco and liquor and keeping warm and fed.' His eyes were as cold as wet river stones." Not many Christian martyrs were so pure in spirit and had so few temptations. Perceiving this quality in another of Jim's statements, Doc Burton remarks, "Pure religious ecstasy. Partakers of the blood of the lamb." When he is killed, Jim does not have a chance to say "You don't know what you're doing"; he and Mac are ambushed and his head is blown off by a shotgun at close range, so that Mac finds him in a still kneeling posture and exclaims simply, "Oh, Christ!" Beginning with the book's title, epigraph, and numerous details taken from *Paradise Lost,* to the crowing of cocks and several allusions to the Holy Family (two of them pointed out by the characters themselves), clearly the committed hero is presented as an imitation of Christ.

Steinbeck's next published novel, *Of Mice and Men* (1937) offers a serious temptation and several pitfalls to anyone dealing with these two themes of escape and commitment. It could be used to illustrate the escape theme by pointing out the persistent dream of George and Lennie to get a place of their own; and even the mercy killing of Lennie by George could be seen as providing Lennie with permanent escape from a world with which he cannot cope, into the dream of the little house and a couple of acres, and rabbits. Or, by concentrating on George, and reading Lennie as a symbol of proletarian man, great in strength but helpless without leadership, the theme of commitment could be seen in George's sacrifices and devotion to Lennie. Or, by bringing out both of these patterns, the novelette could be made to illustrate the nice *balancing* of these two themes. But the escape theme in *Of Mice and Men* is essentially different from the "drop-out" kind of rebellion against society which concerns us here, and is clearly an illusion besides. The commitment is also questionable in its nature and intention. On one level, Lennie is necessary to George as an excuse for his own failure. Admitting *Of Mice and Men* to the present discussion would open the door for numerous other pieces, such as almost all the chapters of *The Pastures of Heaven* and some stories of *The Long Valley,* such as "Flight," most obviously.

But in 1939, with *The Grapes of Wrath*, Steinbeck clearly returns to his theme of social commitment, utilizing, even more extensively than before, pertinent Judeo-Christian analogues and references. It is more than personal friendship that causes Jim Casy to give himself up to the deputies in place of Tom Joad and Floyd. It is an action consequent upon his turning from an individualistic, sin and hell-fire, Bible-belt evangelism to a revelation of the Holy Spirit, which he comes to identify with "all men and all women," the "human sperit—the whole shebang. Maybe all men got one big soul ever'body's a part of." And it occurs to him then that his commitment is not to Jesus but to the people; "An' sometimes I love 'em fit to bust. . . ." This love finally expresses itself in his activities as a labor organizer, devoted to a vision of the Holy Spirit's kingdom on earth, so that he dies saying, twice, "You don' know what you're doin'."

The movement from escape to commitment is even clearer in Tom Joad. He enters the novel determined to avoid all involvement: "I'm laying my dogs down one at a time" and "I climb fences when I got fences to climb." But through the experiences of the migration and through Casy's words and deeds he becomes converted and committed to a vision of social justice beyond hope of his personal experience. Even more than Jim of *In Dubious Battle*, he knows that although he may be killed, "I'll be ever'where—wherever you look. Wherever there's a fight so hungry people can eat, I'll be there. Wherever they's a cop beatin' up a guy, I'll be there. If Casy knowed, why, I'll be in the way guys yell when they're mad an'—I'll be in the way kids laugh when they're hungry an' they know supper's ready. An when our folks eat the stuff they raise an' live in the houses they build—why I'll be there." Beyond this mystic identification, no commitment can go. It is a commitment which gains strength and approval not only by means of its sacrificial Christ figures, but by a wealth of Judeo-Christian references extending from Exodus, Deuteronomy, Canticles and Prophets through John the Baptist, Gospels, and Revelation. *The Grapes of Wrath* is the high point in Steinbeck's theme of commitment. Two years later, in *The Forgotten Village*, a documentary film about Mexican village life, he still stresses commitment by having the young boy, Juan Diego, disobey his parents in bringing his little sister for an inoculation. At the end of the film he leaves home altogether, not to escape, but to go to the city and be trained to better serve and enlighten his people.

The Moon Is Down, Steinbeck's first piece of fiction during the war, has as one of its important characters Mayor Orden. In his refusal to play quisling to the occupying enemy, and his execution for his continuing faith in a democratic society, Mayor Orden might be seen as another of Steinbeck's committed characters. But his commitment is to preserving the present society rather than to creating the future one, and the choice is thrust upon him; actually, compliance would have likewise resulted in death—by his own people. Also, he is not supported by Christian allusions and symbols, as are all the other committed characters, but only with a slight reference to Socrates' *Apology* in the last scene. It is not fruitful to discuss this work at greater length, as the theme of commitment is shared by all but one of the conquered people and it is confused with patriotism and winning the war. In this sense, the enemy, too, is committed, except for one, who wishes to escape. As in the case of *Of Mice and Men*, the relevance to the purpose here is superficial and essentially misleading.

In December of 1944, shortly after returning from a tour of duty as European war correspondent, Steinbeck published *Cannery Row*. With this novel Steinbeck turns once more to the theme of escape as treated in the last novel before his brief proletarian excursion—escape on the level of an entire community of "drop-outs." However, whereas the author of *Tortilla Flat* had accepted its inhabitants with an amused, slightly tongue-in-cheek air, the author of *Cannery Row* several times steps stage-front to proselytize his readers:

> Mack and the boys . . . are the Virtues, the Graces, the Beauties of the hurried mangled craziness of Monterey and the cosmic Monterey where men in fear and hunger destroy their stomachs in the fight to secure certain food, where men hunger-

ing for love destroy everything loveable about them. . . . In the world ruled by tigers with ulcers, rutted by strictured bulls, scavenged by blind jackals, Mack and the boys dine delicately with the tigers, fondle the frantic heifers, and wrap up the crumbs to feed the sea gulls of Cannery Row. What can it profit a man to gain the whole world and to come to his property with a gastric ulcer, a blown prostate, and bifocals? Mack and the boys avoid the trap, walk around the poison, step over the noose while a generation of trapped, poisoned, and trussed-up men scream at them and call them no-goods, come-to-bad-ends, blots-on-the-town, thieves and rascals, bums.

The transfer of Christian reference from the committed characters of his proletarian fiction to these "drop-outs" is significant. In another passage, he calls Mack and the boys "Saints and angels and martyrs and holy men." The ground for these judgments had been indicated three years earlier in *Sea of Cortez*: " . . . of the good we think always of wisdom, tolerance, kindliness, generosity, humility; and the qualities of cruelty, greed, self-interest, graspingness, and rapacity are universally considered undesirable. And yet in our structure of society, the so-called and considered good qualities are invariably concomitants of failure, while the bad ones are the cornerstone of success." It was probably disagreement with this premise that caused one well-known reviewer to say that *Cannery Row* is "a sentimental glorification of weakness of mind and degeneration of character." And so in a sense it is, if one accepts a Kiwanis, Rotary Club, Chamber of Commerce definition of noble character. Perhaps Steinbeck's original suspicions of such a definition were intensified by his experiences in the last years of the Depression and the war which was necessary to end it.

Whatever the reasons, this mood was strong enough to carry over into a variation on the theme in *The Pearl*, originally published in the same year. Strictly speaking, perhaps, this novelette, like *Of Mice and Men* and *The Moon Is Down*, enters only peripherally in this discussion. The pearl diver Kino does seek to physically escape an economically and socially repressive society, but only so that he may return to that same society at a higher level. He can be seen, in his struggle to escape, as what the author of *Cannery Row* called a "tiger with ulcers." And he arrives within reach of his goal with much worse than "a blown prostate and bifocals." He arrives with his house burned down, his wife physically beaten, his only son killed, and the lives of three men on his soul. And then Kino and his wife make their true "escape." They return to their village, throw the Pearl of Great Price back into the sea, and return to the edge of unconsciousness, an unthinking existence governed by the rhythms of sun and tide.

In its interesting variation on the theme of escape, *The Pearl* looks forward to Steinbeck's next novel, published two years later (1947). With this novel Steinbeck finally comes to a resolution of his two themes. Society as pictured in Steinbeck's previous novels is essentially an institutional entity from whose evils a character might decide to escape, or to whose improvement he might dedicate himself. In either case, the monolithic magnitude of the antagonist, society, lent dignity and possible tragedy to his course of action. In *The Wayward Bus,* however, we get very little notion of society as institution; we see it instead as an aggregation of human characters, from the hypocritical businessman, Elliot Pritchard, to Camille Oaks, the honest stripper. Juan Chicoy's decision to escape, therefore, is made in terms of disentanglement from certain people—his neurotic wife and his querulous bus passengers. This, of course, leaves him with no simple distinct notion of direction such as motivated the "drop-outs" and committed characters of Steinbeck's previous fiction. Thus, immediately after abandoning his allegorical bus and its passengers, Juan Chicoy (whose initials are J. C.) becomes merely confused by his escape. "It didn't seem as good or as pleasant or as free" as he had imagined it would. "His nerves itched and he felt mean. . . . Back in the bus he had felt, in anticipation, a bursting orgasmic delight of freedom. But it was not so. He felt miserable. . . . He wondered; 'Won't I ever be happy? Isn't there anything to do?' " So he returns to the bus, as Kino in *The Pearl* returns to his village; but not with a sense of escape or commitment, rather with a sense of involvement without either acceptance or resignation.

Although Steinbeck published five novels after *The Wayward Bus*, the two themes which concern us here play little part in them. *Sweet Thursday* would seem, superficially, a return to the spirit of *Cannery Row* and its glorification of escape, but that escape is so compromised with bourgeois values and genteel spice and color as to become quite respectable. The wonderful whorehouse of *Cannery Row* becomes a school for brides. Doc gets married and accepts a fat research grant at Cal Tech. More interesting is *The Short Reign of Pippin IV*. Pippin is a middle-class Frenchman whose escape is to study the stars rather than society. Then he is discovered to be heir to the throne of a re-established monarchy. In one short speech he presents a seven-point plan of such obvious good sense and modest reasonableness as to antagonize everybody and get himself threatened with the guilliotine. He escapes and returns to his simple home and his telescope (somewhat as Kino returns to his pearl-diving) a contented citizen in a society of corrupt characters. Steinbeck's last novel, *The Winter of Our Discontent*, also touches only peripherally on our topic. The main character, Ethan Hawley, blaming his lack of success in society on his own virtue (as Steinbeck had discussed this relationship in the quotation from *Sea of Cortez*), embarks with deliberate irony upon a course of deviousness which quickly brings him fortune and esteem. In a state of moral shock at his own ability, and that of his children, to adjust so easily to a corrupt society, he attempts a kind of escape through suicide, but allows a contrived excuse to dissuade him. The other two novels of this period, *Burning Bright* and *East of Eden*, do not seem to enter into our topic in any significant way.

What we have, then, in Steinbeck's last novels is neither the individual or communal escapes of his early work and the immediate post-war novels, nor the inspired, Christ-like, sacrificial commitment of his proletarian fiction. Instead, we have a further development of the adjustment made by Juan Chicoy in *The Wayward Bus*. Society continues to be corrupt, although the blame is not so easy to fix; but there is no need for escape or commitment to reform. Steinbeck finally seems to completely accept the observation he had made on marine ecology, in *Sea of Cortez:* "There would seem to be only one commandment for living things: Survive!" This is qualified in *East of Eden* only by a faith in every man's ability to choose between good and evil. This is an old man's wisdom. We continue to read Steinbeck for the folly of his youth.

JOEL W. HEDGPETH

PHILOSOPHY ON CANNERY ROW

It is no easy thing to tell a story plainly and distinctly by mouth; but to tell one on paper is difficult indeed, so many snares lie in the way. People are afraid to put down what is common on paper; they seek to embellish their narratives, as they think, by philosophical speculations and reflections; they are anxious to shine, and people who are anxious to shine can never tell a plain story.

GEORGE BORROW, *Lavengro.*

There is a kind of naturalist . . . who devotes much of his time and energy to the study of nature, doing this because of his love for it and faith in it as that through which his own life and all other lives exist and have meaning and worth.

WILLIAM EMERSON RITTER
and EDNA W. BAILEY,
The Organismal Conception.

I

EDWARD FLANDERS RICKETTS was born in Chicago on May 14, 1897. Most of his childhood was spent in Chicago, and his family background was what might be called undistinguished middle class. The neighborhood on the west side near Garfield Park was, his sister Frances remembered, "deadly respectable, not very good or very bad people, not perhaps very typical of city life. Anyway it was very uninteresting to Ed who loved a little more drama. I suppose that is why he roamed over all the rest of the city. Our early life was spent rather in the shadow of a small Englishy Episcopal church which our parents were pillars of." It does not sound like the environment to produce the sort of naturalist that Ed Ricketts developed into, but more like that to have spawned the literary inclined Donald Culross Peattie, born in Chicago a year later. But boys do wander about the cities they live in, and the little events during such wanderings that may have had a large part in shaping their way of looking at the world are seldom remembered and even less often recorded for the benefit of those who come later. Of course it may have been as Ed himself wrote to a publisher for publicity purposes: "Later on, at the age of 6, I was ruined for any ordinary activities when an uncle who should have known better gave me some natural history curios and an old zoology textbook. Here I saw for the first time those magic and incorrect words 'coral insects'."

According to his sister, "the break in our childhood was one year about 1907-08 which was spent in a small South Dakota town, Mitchell. This was heaven for all three of us children who had never before been allowed out of sight unsupervised by our elders. It must have been most wonderful for Ed, who, besides making his usual warm good contacts with people, collected butterflies on a big scale and birds' eggs a little too avidly. Ed also raised what I thought were enormous flocks of pigeons, and was in love with the rector's daughter, a very advanced vivid girl named Victoria."

Ed began his college career at Illinois State Normal about 1915-1916, where he evidently was introduced to zoology. However, after a year of this he wandered off to Texas and New Mexico, working for a while as an accountant in a country club in El Paso and as a member of a surveying party in New Mexico. He always loved this mountain country and in one of his last journal entries considers making trips out into the desert to develop new ideas. After an uneventful service with the Army (1918-1919) he entered the University of Chicago. The only courses he took seriously were those in zoology, and he helped support himself by working for a very small biological supply house which was really part of a fishing tackle supply company, the Anco Biological Supplies section of the Anglers Company. For some part of his years at Chicago Ed shared quarters with J. Nelson Gowanloch, who became Chief Biologist for the Louisiana Conservation Department in New Orleans (an amiable, cultured biosophist who died not unsurprisingly of cirrhosis of the liver), and Albert E. Galigher, who originally started the biological supply venture at Pacific Grove that brought Ed out to the Pacific Coast as a partner in 1923.

According to a statement from the registrar, "Edward Flanders Ricketts attended the University of Chicago from June 1919 to December 1922. He received no degree from the University." There is no room in the dehydrated records of registrars for significant events beyond bare dates or lists of courses attended, and this meager record omits the most significant event of those years as far as its subject was concerned: the appointment of W. C. Allee to the faculty of the University of Chicago in 1921 and the impression he made upon his students. For several years before he came to Chicago, Allee had conducted a significant project at Woods Hole, and at the time he joined the faculty at Chicago he was engaged in writing this work up and without doubt discussed it in his classes. For every summer from 1915 through 1921 Allee and his students had made systematic collections from characteristic areas of the shore in the vicinity of Woods Hole. The principal physical factors controlling distribution were analyzed, and some of the common associations were recognized. The repetition of observations every year as part of the field trip experience at the seashore has not often been done and still remains the exception, at least insofar as careful record-keeping is concerned, although it is even more essential in this era of environmental concern than it was in Allee's days at Woods Hole.

At the time he came to Chicago, however, Allee was becoming more interested in the nature of associations, and by 1931 had produced his classic work on the subject, *Animal Ag-*

gregations.[1] This work might be considered essentially as an effort to ascertain some basic ecological principle through the study of natural groupings of organisms. Some of Allee's colleagues were of the opinion that he perhaps sought too hard for data in support of his devoutly Quaker convictions about social cooperation as an objective phenomenon in nature. Nevertheless, the ecological way of thinking exemplified in Allee's work inspired many students, and ultimately resulted in one of the great classics of ecology, the monumental *Principles of Animal Ecology* by Allee, Emerson, Park, Park, and Schmidt (1949), for a time known as "the great AEPPS (apes)." But that was to be three decades later. In the concluding section of *Animal Aggregations* there are such paragraphs as the following:

> It may be that numerous transitions from the non-living to the living would occur one after the other in the same microniche, with a successive conditioning and a progressively greater longevity of some or all of the particles, until finally conditions would become sufficiently favorable for permanent survival. Whatever the details, it seems probable that this mechanism was operative from the very beginning of life and is a fundamental trait or property of living matter.
>
> In order to discuss this trait more easily, it should be named. A few years ago it might have been called "unconscious co-operation"; but since many modern psychologists have discarded the concept of consciousness, the idea of lack of consciousness is less helpful than formerly. It may be regarded as an automatic mutual interdependence among organisms, or, for the sake of simplicity, as the principle of co-operation. The only trouble with calling this relationship one of co-operation, which it is, lies in the fact that the word carries with it an idea of conscious effort . . . possible only after long ages of organic evolution, and then only in certain favored types of animals, while the evidence appears to be clear that the sort of co-operation of which we are speaking is a fundamental trait of living matter. As in all the other fundamental properties of living organisms, there is probably no hard and fast line to be drawn here between the living and the non-living. The mutual interdependence of the living must have grown out of similar but simpler interdepend-

---

[1] W. C. Allee, *Animal Aggregations*, (Chicago, 1931).

ence in antecedent non-living matter, and may, in fact, be merely a highly specialized biological application of the mass law of chemistry.

If this analysis be sound, as it appears to be, the potentiality of social life is inherent in living matter, even though its first manifestations are merely those of a slight mutual interdependence, or of an automobile co-operation which finds its first biological expression as a subtle binding link of primitive ecological biocoenoses. Lest we be accused of having been carried too far by enthusiasm, it may be well to pause for a moment to examine the extent to which this automatic co-operation has been demonstrated to exist among animals. Are we, in fact, dealing with a phenomenon known to be sufficiently widespread to be thought of as having general rather than special biological significance? (354-356).

In addition to the group survival values known to be so widely distributed among animals, taxonomically considered, we have seen that similar survival values have been demonstrated for such diverse organisms as bacteria, for the spermatozoa of several kinds of aquatic animals and of mammals, and for tissue-culture cells. Evidently mutual interdependence, or automatic co-operation, is sufficiently widespread among the animal kingdom to warrant the conclusion given above that it ranks as one of the fundamental qualities of animal protoplasm, and probably of protoplasm in general (357).

Ed took to these ideas, kept them, and thought them over for the rest of his life—one of the last entries in his notebooks is a reference to Allee's ideas being misused by the communists, and the underlying philosophy of his work on the seashore can best be characterized by the concluding sentence of *Animal Aggregations:*

It has been much more easy for a student beginning with the humbler group levels to follow, from the social beginnings which he learns to recognize in almost unintegrated animal aggregations, the possibilities of the development of great social structures; and to trace their growth slowly and as yet imperfectly, but surely.

The impression that Allee made upon Ed was equal to that made on the teacher by his student, for 29 years later Allee could write:

I know Edward F. Ricketts' and Jack Calvin's "Between Pacific Tides" and respect it. Mr. Ricketts' death was a shock for I had expected him to go much further.

In regard to your request for reminiscences or impressions I may have had of Edward F. Ricketts, I first met him on becoming a staff member at the University of Chicago in 1921. He was a member of a small group of "Ishmaelites" who tended sometimes to be disturbing, but were always stimulating. I am pleased, particularly that Mr. Ricketts lived up to the promise he showed in those years of having real ability.

(W.C.A. to J.W.H., Sept. 18, 1950)

The kind of ecology that Ed learned from Allee was comparatively unknown on the Pacific Coast in 1923, and Ed brought it with him when he came to Pacific Grove to be a partner in the biological supply business with A. E. Galigher. It is possible that Ed, still remembering some of the details about Allee's Woods Hole work, lost no time in looking at the California seashore at low tide, in the region described by Allee: " . . . in such favorable locations as part of the California coast, the supply of life is appalling. One cannot step on the rocks exposed at low tide without crushing sea urchins, sea anemones, barnacles, or mollusks." (*Animal Aggregations*, p. 358). "Appalling" is a most uncharacteristic word for a biologist to use, incidentally.

In the summer of the year that Ed Ricketts came to Pacific Grove, John Steinbeck attended Hopkins Marine Station. Years later he told Rolf Bolin, a professor at Hopkins Marine Station, that the most memorable idea he got from that summer at the seashore was the concept of the superorganism:

I gained the impression that his Marine Station experience was a real eye-opener, but the only specific idea that he ever indicated to me as resulting from it was the concept of a group of individuals acting as a superorganism in the same way that an individual acts as a supercell. Although this idea is a keystone in modern ecology, it was fairly new then, I believe, and I was first struck by it in discussions with John.

(R.L.B. to J.W.H., March 24, 1970)

In the margin of the letter Dr. Bolin noted: "Perhaps he got this from Ed after all." Perhaps. It is difficult to trace the origin of ideas through ex post facto recollections. Steinbeck did attend the summer session of 1923 at the marine station and at that time he took the formal general zoology course from C. V. Taylor, a student of Charles A. Kofoid at Berkeley. This was in the days when William Emerson Ritter of the University of California was expounding his ideas of the organismal conception: " . . . in all parts of nature and in nature itself as one gigantic whole, wholes are so related to their parts that not only does the existence of the whole depend on the orderly cooperation and interdependence of its parts, but the whole exercises a measure of determinative control over its parts."[2] This was an extrapolation of Ritter's studies of ascidians, colonial animals in which the functional individuals form a unit, often of discrete and characteristic shape, which are a natural indication that a whole may be greater than the sum of its parts. Ritter's interest in this topic had led him to write a two-volume work on the subject which was published in 1919 (*The Unity of the Organism or The Organismal Conception of Life*). As Ritter points out, the extension of this idea to human society is not new, and the theory of society as an organism was particularly identified with Herbert Spencer.

It should not be overlooked that Ritter was concerned with individuals or cells of a species forming larger groups, not with the idea of an assemblage of different kinds of organisms forming a larger organism. Allee was careful not to suggest more than that there was a tendency for organisms to live together in various combinations and that such associations appeared to have survival value for the individual kinds of organisms involved. While this may be a useful analogy for sociologists, it is not the same thing as colonial growth forms made up of individuals of a species, some of them actually differentiated and

---

[2] William E. Ritter and Edna W. Bailey, "The Organismal Conception. Its Place in Science and Its Bearing on Philosophy," *Univ. Calif. Publ. Zoology*, XXXI, (1928), 307-358.

specialized to serve the common purpose of the colony. A. E. Emerson, a colleague of Allee's and a specialist in termites, carried speculation about aggregations on to suggest that an ant or termite colony functioned as a single organism and might be considered a sort of superorganism. It would appear at this late date that what Steinbeck was thinking of (*fide* Rolf Bolin) was closer to Ritter's idea than to Allee's, as might be expected if he was introduced to it by an instructor trained at Berkeley where such ideas were part of the Zeitgeist of the Department of Zoology at the time. However, the strong cast of Allee as transmitted by Ricketts shows up in Steinbeck's writing more clearly than the formal zoological concept based on cells and the individual members of a colonial organism. Quite possibly, Ricketts introduced Allee's book to Steinbeck early in their friendship. Unfortunately many of Ricketts' personal papers and notes were destroyed in the fire that burned down his original laboratory in 1936, so it is unlikely that this may be confirmed.

In a tantalizing scrap of paper, obviously part of a carbon copy of a letter, Ricketts wrote: "I have been especially interested in John Steinbeck's notions because they developed widely the holistic concepts being felt specifically in modern biology. The zoologist Allee must be interested in these enlarged horizons which might very easily (altho I happen to know they couldn't) have sprung from the germ of his animal aggregation concept. Many workers in the vanguard of science and the arts achieve independently expression of the same underlying concept."

In any event it is obvious that Steinbeck's interest in marine biology did not arise out of his association with Ed Ricketts, as Fontenrose seems to suggest.[3] Indeed, the friendship with Ricketts probably developed in part out of a common interest in biology. What remains unexplained, so far, is how Steinbeck

---

[3] Joseph Fontenrose, *John Steinbeck: An Introduction and Interpretation* (New York, 1963), p. 5.

became interested enough in biology to take courses at Stanford and spend a summer at the marine station. He might have been attracted to Hopkins Marine Station not only because it was near home but also because during the summer of 1923 courses in English composition and literature were also offered (unusual fare for a marine station, but it would be a good thing if the idea were revived). But Steinbeck did not enroll for English but for general zoology.[4] It is curious how meager the published information about Steinbeck is, especially in this matter of his early interest in biology. Salinas, a country town in the days of Steinbeck's boyhood, was, like most parts of incompletely urbanized California of fifty or sixty years ago, never far from nature and Steinbeck's close affinity for nature expressed in so many ways in his writing reflects this out-of-doors background. It is much more natural to expect a boy from this background to become interested in biology than one from the streets of Chicago.

Edward F. Ricketts and John Steinbeck met in a dentist's waiting room in 1930. They had heard of each other, and Steinbeck recalled in his profile *About Ed Ricketts,* that he had wanted to meet him for some time, but that he was shy about it because Ed was making about a hundred to one hundred fifty a month in his business. (He had parted ways with Galigher, who moved to Berkeley with the prepared slide part of the business, and so was the owner of the Pacific Biological Laboratories. The falling out with Galigher was a result of conflict of interest in the same woman.) In these days of debased money values we must be reminded that during the Depression people could get married and save money on a hundred a month.

By 1930, Ricketts' interest in seashore life had reached the stage where he was working with Jack Calvin on the original

---

[4] Steinbeck might have been attracted by the statement on page nine of the *Hopkins Marine Station Bulletin* for 1923: "The particular advantage of work at the Station is the possibility of observing and studying a large number of live animals while these are still fulfilling their role in the general scheme of marine and terrestrial life."

draft of *Between Pacific Tides.* This work led him to examine the phenomenon of the tides, as associated with the occurrence of life on the seashore, in considerable detail. Although Ricketts never published this study, he completed a paper on it sometime around 1934-1935; at least the copy in the Hopkins Marine Station acknowledges the Tide Tables for 1934 and the actual data for 1931. This essay, titled "The Tide as an Environmental Factor Chiefly with Reference to Ecological Zonation on the California Coast," was made freely available to Willis G. Hewatt, a graduate student at Hopkins Marine Station who conducted his thesis research at Hopkins Marine Station from October 1931 to June 1933, with supplemental observations in 1934, and to Torsten Gislén, a visiting Swedish investigator who made comparative studies of the shores of Japan and California. Gislén was at Hopkins Marine Station from December 1930 to April 1931. During the last days of February and first days of March of 1931 Gislén visited Southern California and Baja California as far as Ensenada; he was taken there by "Mr. E. F. Ricketts of Pacific Grove, who arranged our trip along the California coast down into Mexico." Both Hewatt and Gislén made considerable use of Ricketts' manuscript and acknowledged their indebtedness to him.[5] Hewatt's condensed thesis, published in 1937, contains two of the graphs compiled by Ricketts. Gislén's papers on his California studies were not published until 1943 and 1945, but his indebtedness to Ricketts was extensive and fully acknowledged. A very small part of this interesting and still significant essay was used in *Between Pacific Tides.*

Ricketts considered this paper unpublishable because of the loss of notes in the fire of 1936, although parts of it are still original and the paper as a whole forms the scientific basis for his fourfold division of the Pacific intertidal zones. Certainly the paper would have been of great use to me in revising *Between*

---

[5] These references are cited and discussed in appropriate parts of *Between Pacific Tides.*

Pacific Tides, but at that time nobody seemed to know where a copy was.

The essay on the tide was not the only unpublished effort that Ed made available to his friends. There were several philosophical essays, preliminary prefaces to projected works, and the like. These included the essay on nonteleological thinking that found its way into *Sea of Cortez* and two others—"The Philosophy of Breaking Through" and "A Spiritual Morphology of Poetry." Some of these he sent around to such magazines as *Harper's* and *Atlantic,* and collected rejection slips for his pains. One essay was published, actually a narrative account of his walking trip from Indianapolis to Savannah in the winter of 1921 (evidently he started out in November by train from Chicago to Indianapolis). According to the published account (*Travel,* June 1925) he had worked too hard at the University and at earning his living and hit upon the idea of a long hike as a welcome change, but actually he had had an upsetting love affair. The article reflects Ed's characteristic interest in people and their ways, and ends with an account of listening to spirituals being sung in a Savannah cemetery one morning after a storm. The article ends as if there were more to come; either another installment was intended or the editor cut it short.

Steinbeck describes this episode in Ed's life in *Cannery Row:*

> . . . Once when Doc was at the University of Chicago he had love trouble and he had worked too hard. He thought it would be nice to take a very long walk. He put on a little knapsack and he walked through Indiana and Kentucky and North Carolina and Georgia clear to Florida. He walked among farmers and mountain people, among the swamp people and fishermen. And everywhere people asked him why he was walking through the country.
>
> Because he loved true things he tried to explain. He said he was nervous and besides he wanted to see the country, smell the ground and look at grass and birds and trees, to savor the country, and there was no other way to do it save on foot. And people didn't like him for telling the truth. They scowled, or shook and tapped their heads, they laughed as though they knew it was a

lie and they appreciated a liar. And some, afraid for their daughters or their pigs, told him to move on, to get going, just not to stop near their place if he knew what was good for him.

And so he stopped trying to tell the truth. He said he was doing it on a bet—that he stood to win a hundred dollars. Everyone liked him then and believed him. They asked him in to dinner and gave him a bed and they put lunches up for him and wished him good luck and thought he was a hell of a fine fellow. Doc still loved true things but he knew it was not a general love and it could be a very dangerous mistress.

This concept of "true things" was central with Ed Ricketts. In his notebooks he wrote often of the "deep thing" or the "true thing." He also had a strong drive for work, and to the extent that this aspect of him is underemphasized Steinbeck's profile is inaccurate, and the portrait of Doc in *Cannery Row* is a pastiche, although Steinbeck did remark on Ed's antlike methodical restoration of his laboratory after the fire of 1936. In his notebook for sometime in 1942, Ed attempts a self portrait:

> Anyone who truly has "work to do" in the (outer) world will get to admiring Goethe's dictum "Haste not, waste not." The lucky ones who are physically and emotionally relaxed so that they can just "be"—and enjoy life—need not have (more than enough to keep them economically adjusted and psychol. adj. to a world that respects some significant outside world) but the rest of the really worth while people have to "work" to build a business, a concept, a work of art, or an organization, they have to create something externally. Because I am relaxed enough to enjoy life, leisure, dawdling around talking or laughing, only once or twice a week, I must put in the rest of my life working hard and unceasingly and taking considerable exercise, if I am to avoid ill health, irritation and frustration. . . . I am usually too tense to be able to sit around enjoyably, lovingly, and listen to people talk and laugh and myself participate. I have to be up and doing. If I were well and often screwed, I could participate in the joy of life. Then I have better extroversion, more confidence, I could then do things like dancing and swimming and just loafing around, building my inner happiness and balance that will radiate around and affect an increasing circle with true life and (mainly psychic) works. But I'm not so intense. So I have to put just about all my considerable energy, not in living,

but in doing and in doing wisely not frantically. I have to utilize every hour and in missionary for my way of life. Otherwise I'll get bored. "Haste not, waste not."

On the opp. side the life usually thot of as "dolce far niente" may not represent either the desideratum mentioned above in connection with the balanced external life "haste not, waste not," or it may represent the sort of degeneration that overtakes the business man who puts everything in his business—into his persona—with the loss of all his internals. A South Sea island beachcomber who starts out with the real deep thing (relationally say, with a native woman, or with a region) can degenerate into a true loafer, a non-entity, a complete loss, he can have nought but leisure, just as a business man can degenerate into a non-entity, even tho amassing a fortune. I could have a real deep true life either way relationally thru relaxation with such a person as X — — — or as X — — — might have been, or externally thru zoology and construct of deep true manuals. Having both would be ideal and theoret. not impossible. But practically not advisable. . . .

My own acquaintance with Ed Ricketts began through correspondence about the pycnogonids to be included in *Between Pacific Tides* in 1935, but I did not meet him until one afternoon late in 1938, or perhaps early in 1939. I presented myself unannounced, and he opened the door and hesitated a startled second before inviting me in. We were the same size and had similar beards, and he was wearing a wool plaid shirt. Perhaps I was also; I do not remember. I do not remember much else about that meeting or much about some of the other times I called, except that one time when I was there Ed had the advance galleys of *The Grapes of Wrath* and predicted it would win the Pulitzer Prize. In 1941, Ed began to discuss plans for a revised edition of *Between Pacific Tides* and I agreed to prepare some diagrams and an end paper map. The map was never used, but I later prepared a new version for the third edition. For several years I visited Pacific Grove two or three times a year, and seldom met anyone else at Ed's place except Steinbeck (who studied me at first like some sort of bug, I thought), and became involved in a couple of parties which I very dimly remember.

I am an incomplete and sporadic journal keeper, but I do find this entry, for December 28, 1939: "Pacific Grove.—In which I meet John Steinbeck, a bluff hearty fellow, who collected a pycnogonid at Bolinas last week [actually it was on Christmas Day, according to the label]—a new distribution record for *Nymphopsis spinossimus*. Biologists, he said, were the tenors of science. . . . Ricketts and I discussed everything from biology to art to music, winding up with Monteverdi on the phonograph when interrupted by Mrs. Steinbeck and a gallon of wine. I would have liked to have heard more of the Monteverdi. He is starting a new book with Steinbeck on invertebrates for high school use, which should be useful indeed."

I last saw Ed on February 6, 1945, when I was on my way to Rockport, Texas, to become a marine biologist for the Texas Game Fish and Oyster Commission (I had given up trying to make my way as a hack writer on nature subjects; I find in my files that in 1941 I tried to establish with the *San Francisco Chronicle* the sort of job that Harold Gilliam now fills). I stayed overnight at the lab and Ed was entranced by the Byrd *Mass for Five Voices* which he had just got. He was fascinated by the thought that the choir that performed it was the descendant of the original choir directed by William Byrd, so there was a living tradition of interpretation. I was fascinated by the music, and he promised to send me a copy. This he had made, perhaps at some expense, and it consoled me in the dreary wastes of the Texas coast. I still have it. We corresponded actively during my years in exile, but I never saw him again, for he was away when I returned for brief visits. I returned permanently to the Pacific coast in 1949, and in 1950 was approached by the Stanford Press to assume the task of preparing a new edition of *Between Pacific Tides*.

I never knew what to expect on those visits to Cannery Row, nor, I suppose, did anyone else. That was part of Ed's charm. He might be all fired up with speculations about Bach's tuning of the diatonic scale, or would want to discuss why geniuses occurred in clusters (there was a big chart like one of those histogram affairs for cramming students on the wall in 1945) or why our exasperating colleague Jinglebollix could write such poor descriptions of animals (especially pycnogonids), and at the same time be an effective teacher. I wish I had known him better, but I lived too far away to become part of the circle.

It seems to me that the most characteristic thing about Ed was his interest in communicating with people, and in his notebook I find verification of this;

> Re my concern over the deep things in sex or love or friendship or thinking or esthetics not being communicated: It gives me a feeling a waste, of futility, when I have the spark and cannot communicate it. I get frustrated and negativistic.
>
> Now I suppose I have to work that out so that I myself am not constricted or diminished by not being able to "get across." Fr inst I used to have my own appreciation of music but when a fellow listener wasn't appreciative, just as my appreciation was heightened or sent into interesting new channels by the appreciation of a fellow listener. But I have finally got to the point where what I have (which is good) isn't completely squelched by non-appreciation to which I'm subjected. (July 18, Sunday 1942).

There was evidently a great deal of personal association as well as what might be called abstract esthetics in Ed's appreciation of music, incidentally. I think that Ed and I were in agreement, at least in 1945, that great music ended with Bach. He was most interested in choral music, although, as Steinbeck noted, he could not sing. He did not have the kind of voice that could carry a sustained tone, and probably could not have been trained to do so, although a vignette in a folder for a proposed essay labeled "Nostalgia" concerns his introduction to choral music as a choir boy:

> When I remember a church cantata once I sung, as a child, I get a sense of haunting loveliness which it would be easy to tie up with the music. It was a good time in my life; I was very much ten-year-old in love with that good Ethel. The new snow was on the ground when I walked home with her; we dragged behind the others; doesn't matter what we said,

perhaps nothing, maybe we just walked along silently in brilliance. But there aren't any words for what that was. It was a very *real* thing too. Now I tend to invest that thing in her, and more in the music. It was real enough, but it was *not* she, nor I. We only were cloaked with it (altho I know of course it came from us) but it was greater than we were, than we are even now. And particularly it wasn't the music. We merely invested the music with it. And I can bring that thing back faintly anytime, merely by remembering the time. Actually the music was very second rate. In spite of the nostalgia I'm certain of that. And now I'm clear enough so that an outsider could belittle or even ridicule the music without bothering me. I know it's fit only for ridicule. But what we put in it was the real thing.

It's particularly fortunate for me that my wonderful glow got tied up with music so inconsequential. Think if that had been a Bach Cantata! I mightn't ever get clear. Now I have to face the fact that the important thing isn't the inconsequential music. What's important is what I projected into it.

II

Between Pacific Tides, the book that was to establish Ed Ricketts' reputation as a seashore biologist, had its origins as a sort of cottage industry among a group of people at Pacific Grove during the Depression. Ed's friends, who enjoyed going with him on low tide collecting trips, encouraged him to write all these things up. In the beginning it was to be a little book for beginners, and Jack Calvin, a struggling free-lance writer of Sunday school stories and the like, would help make the writing intelligible for the layman. Calvin would also take the photographs, and his brother-in-law, Ritchie Lovejoy, would prepare some drawings.[6] The scope of the book grew and grew and by

---

[6] Jack Calvin and Ritchie Lovejoy married two of the daughters of Father Andri Kashevaroff of Juneau. Since there is a popular myth developing along the waterfront that Ed Ricketts and John Steinbeck were married to Kashevaroff sisters, the following vital statistics concerning Father Kashevaroff's family, as provided by Jack Calvin (Oct. 10, 1970), seem necessary:

> The first born was the only boy, Cyril, dead these many years. Next came a girl who was killed in childhood by a runaway horse. After that, in order, came Sasha, who married me before she knew

mid-1930 there was enough of it to send to publishers for consideration. The going was hard: eastern publishers were not interested in western regional books; sales of Johnson and Snook's *Seashore Animals of the Pacific Coast* (Macmillan, 1927) were slow and the subsidy by Ellen Browning Scripps was probably the main reason that book was published at all.

In a letter to the Stanford University Press accompanying a prospectus, signed by E. F. Ricketts and dated June 27, 1930, the ecological format of the work was defined. It would have the virtues of (a) novelty, (b) ease of application by ordinary tourist and observer, and (c) enhanced quick value even to the scientist and serious student. Reference was also made to more detailed bibliographic information to save students many days searching the literature, "especially where, as at the Hopkins Marine Station, there is no reference to papers relating to Monterey Bay forms." The basic organization, the approach by the various types of seashore habitat, including exposed and protected shore, was modeled upon a paper by W. C. Allee which appeared in *Biological Bulletin* in two installments in 1923.[7] This work is starred in the bibliography of the first edition of *Between Pacific Tides* as "indispensable," with this annotation:

Ed; then Nadja, widow of LeRoy Vestal, now married to Holly Triplette; then Legia, who married Brewer, then John Olson, and died about five years ago; then Natalya, who came to Carmel to visit us and married Ritchie Lovejoy, a protege of mine at the time. The Lovejoys stayed on after we left, and stayed married to each other. He died some years ago; she died last year. The last was Xenia, who lived with Sasha and me for a year and attended Monterey High School. She went east, was married to John Cage for several years, has not remarried.

[7] W. C. Allee, *Studies in Marine Ecology: 1* (1923). The distribution of common littoral invertebrates of the Woods Hole Region. *Biol. Bull.* IVL (4): 167-191; III. Some physical factors related to the distribution of littoral invertebrates. *Ibid.*, (5): 205-253.

Part II was never published; it is (was) an annotated catalogue, deposited with the U. S. Fish Commission Library at Woods Hole. Copies were to be sent to several other institutions including "Scripps Institution at La Jolla," but I never found it there.

"One of the few comprehensive treatments of a restricted area in this country. Although concerned with the fauna of Woods Hole, it pictures a state of affairs applicable anywhere."

The original referee for the Stanford Press was not, obviously, ready for the Woods Hole or Chicago approach, for he stated in a letter of December 2, 1931 (evidently the book was completed by then):

> I read the manuscript with somewhat mixed emotions. The facts are authentic so far as I could see and on the whole it was fairly well written, barring a certain vulgarity in places which doubtless can be eliminated by the Editor. The method of taking up the animals from the standpoint of station and exposure on the seashore seems at first sight very logical but from the practical standpoint it seems to me not particularly happy. . . . Certain zoological keys could be inserted which might overcome to a large extent this difficulty. After all, the end aim of a book of this sort is to answer the question "What is it?". After this the reader is concerned with habits, etc.

This dour opinion by the late Walter K. Fisher stalled things for five years, but the book would not die, or its authors refused to give up and it was evidently resubmitted late in 1935 (by this time Calvin had moved to Alaska). In a letter of February 29, 1936, Dr. Fisher stated (among other things) that "the MS needs rigorous editing but not by the author, who will be hampered by unfortunate limitations in the use of English. There is some good ecology scattered through the work. I think the book will make the grade if aimed at high school teachers and students . . . the book will be useful for a well educated layman *at the seashore* (but not in his "arm-chair"). From what I have said you may perhaps infer that I do not think particularly well of the MS. As a matter of fact I think Ricketts (a collector rather than a trained biologist) has done very well indeed. Only he doesn't realize his limitations and that he has undertaken a very difficult job."

Apparently this somewhat diffident endorsement was enough to encourage the Stanford Press to accept the book for publication in 1936. But all was not smooth sailing, for there were obviously objections to the "Annotated Systematic Index and Bibliography." The advice of Professor S. F. Light of the University of California was solicited as to the value of this appendix, with its implications of trouble in the print shop with all sorts and sizes of type. Probably Ed suggested Dr. Light. Interestingly enough, Light's endorsement of the appendix was written during a summer session at Moss Beach where he was holding his famous Zoology 112 course. There was nothing like it available, wrote Dr. Light: " . . . I can assure you that it will be of very great value, will be very much used and will inevitably lead to increased investigation in the areas involved. It would be a *very great misfortune* if this material were to be omitted." (June 6, 1937.) He then offered to send some additional material. It is my own memory that Dr. Light did not think too much of some of the text and after the book was published considered the appendix its most valuable part. But he did prove a better prophet than Dr. Fisher, whose viewpoint on many things was somewhat astringent.

Finally, *Between Pacific Tides* appeared in 1939. A thousand copies were printed, and the book lapsed from print from 1942 to 1948, when the second, or revised edition appeared a few months after the death of Ed Ricketts. The publishing history of the various editions is appended to this paper.

No one realized more than Ed Ricketts that *Between Pacific Tides* needed much improvement, and early in 1941 he was discussing revisions with the Stanford Press. The work on the revised edition was not completed until just before Ed's death, and included a chapter on plankton. Unfortunately the information available was not adequate for the sort of analysis that was attempted, and it has been necessary to discard this effort from later editions.

Between Pacific Tides was hardly published before Ed began to think about a book of narrowed geographic scope, a handbook of marine invertebrates of the San Francisco Bay area. A draft for a preface to this proposed work is among his papers at Hopkins Marine Station. "It will be specifically designed for beginning biology classes but will be written and ordered so that it may be used by the sea coast wanderer who finds interest in the little bugs and would like to know what they are and how they live." Although it is not stated in the draft, this was evidently for the joint project with Steinbeck that he mentioned to me the preceding December; some pages are dated January 7, others August 27, 1940.

Toward the end of this draft introduction, after a discussion of the various physical factors and the biological interactions between individuals and groups, there are two paragraphs of particular interest:

> The sociological complex resulting from all these interplays has been at the same time engaged in maintaining a balance with respect to its communal and individual threshholds to the physical factors previously enumerated, so that the whole represents a delicate equilibrium of the most complex sort. This is fairly comparable to the social and economic inter-relations within that species we consider highest of all animals. In this connection, note the relations between individuals, families, friends, races, and nations, which involve expediences both political (power-drive), emotional and economic (hunger and poverty), with their ideologies, competitions, needs, overproductions, overpopulations and wars. Most of these have their primitive counterparts along the shore. Who would see a replica of man's social structure has only to examine the abundant and various life of the tidepools, where miniature communal societies wage dubious battle against equally potent societies in which the individual is paramount, with trends shifting, maturing, or dying out, with all the living organisms balanced against the limitations of the dead kingdom of rocks and currents and temperatures and dissolved gases. A study of animal communities has this advantage: they are merely what they are, for anyone to see who will and can look clearly; they cannot complicate the picture by worded idealisms, by saying one thing and being another; here the struggle is unmasked and the beauty is unmasked.

> Even the two chief philosophies of human society are paralleled on the shore: those dedicated to the principle that the individual serves the state, chiefly as a unit or cog in that suprapersonal social organization that is the colony; and those based on the democratic principle that the state serves the all-important

individual. The latter are exemplified by the octopus and by other actively predacious animals which, by their individual skill through intelligence and sensory ability, function as free entities; the former by the sponges, corals, barnacles, compound tunicates, etc., which very definitely function as a group in competitive food getting, in colonizing every available square inch of suitable area, and in reproducing, and in which the colonial individual is almost entirely lost sight of before the coherent unity of the community.

The project never got beyond this introduction, probably because S. F. Light's "Laboratory and Field Text in Invertebrate Zoology" was published in 1941.[8] Ideas were not put down easily, however, and the problem of animal communities as analogs for human societies was seldom far from Ed's mind. He wrote to John Steinbeck, on September 15, 1946: "I am interested now more than ever in comparing the action of human society as is—and how it got there—with the presence of societies in the tidepools, and their controlling environmental factors, but I don't know if I can work it out intelligently, acceptably and interestedly."

Some of the ideas from the draft of 1940 appeared in the chapter on plankton in the revised edition of *Between Pacific Tides* in 1948; the thought about nature being unable to say one thing and be another reappears in the conclusion of this essay:

> Only one large thesis can be stated with any degree of certainty. The idea of hierarchy is implicit. Rank behind rank, societies stand in mutual interdependence. From the most minute and ephemeral bacteria and diatoms, clear up to the fish, seals, and whales, each rank is supported by the abundance of smaller and more transient creatures under it. Each in turn contributes

---

[8] In the Fourth Edition of *Between Pacific Tides* (pp. 540-545) I have compiled a bibliography of all the books on Pacific Coast seashore life that have come to my attention. It should be noted that Muriel Guberlet's *Animals of the Seashore* is also in print (Portland, Metropolitan Press, 1936; later, Binfords & Mort), but an inquiry to the publisher concerning its printing history was not answered. It is simply a series of photographs with short commentaries.

to the series next above it. Ascending ranks have each a little more leeway in the matter of food storage, a little more resilience, a little more freedom of movement in the environment. Although the individuals are larger, their numbers are smaller. And their spores—the resting stages—are less significant in the life history. Finally, at the top of the hierarchy, the disintegrating body of the whale supports astronomical hordes of bacteria, busily engaged in breaking down the complex and slowly assembled proteins into simpler units which fertilize the waters for the oncoming crop of diatoms—James Joyce's *recorso* theme in its original manifestation.

Each higher order, instead of ruling the ranks of individuals below, is actually ruled by them. Each rank is completely at the mercy of its subjects, dependent on their abundance or accessibility. All the schemes which our social order prides itself on having discovered have been in use by societies of marine animals far back into the dim geological past. The units comprising human society very commonly claim to be one thing and are another. Not the least of the many values of marine sociology is the fact that the sea animals can be only themselves. (p. 374).[9]

Between the first version of this introduction to an unwritten book and the plankton chapter of the second edition of *Between Pacific Tides*, however, was interposed the *Sea of Cortez*. Ed Ricketts and John Steinbeck engaged the Western Flyer (charter was not exactly the word for it) for a trip to the Gulf of California during the months of March-April 1940, and worked over the material and Ed's journal of the trip immediately afterward. *Sea of Cortez: A Leisurely Journal of Travel and Research* was published in December of 1941. When one

---

[9] These ideas that animal communities "cannot complicate the picture by worded idealisms, by saying one thing and being another" and that "sea animals can be only themselves" are startlingly similar to a passage in Herman Hesse's *Steppenwolf:* "You must certainly see that all of them are alright, that not a single animal is embarassed or does not know what he should do and how he should behave himself. They do not want to call attention to themselves. No acting. They are what they are, like stones and flowers, or like the stars in heaven."

If there is a common source, it could be Novalis; Ed had the Insel Edition of selected writings of Novalis among his books.

considers the details and miscellaneous correspondence necessary to secure determination of some of the material in the Annotated Phyletic Catalogue and Bibliography, to say nothing of organizing what still remains a unique contribution to the general zoology of the Gulf of California, the pace of the authors was obviously far from leisurely. But the book was not exactly a product of haste, for years of thinking, of bull sessions and unpublished philosophical essays, one at least of them dating back to Ed's student days in Chicago, were added to the fresh experiences of the expedition. Ricketts was seeing some near-tropical environments, although he was never to see the great coral reefs that he someday hoped to, and Steinbeck was conducting himself like a professional zoologist. The result, as Ed wrote to me (Nov. 18, 1941), was a true collaboration:

> However much it seems otherwise, "Sea of Cortez" is truly a compilation. Jon worked at the collecting and sorting of animals, and looked over some of the literature, including the specialist literature, and I had a hand even in the narrative, altho the planning and architecture of the first part of course is entirely his, as the planning of the scientific section is entirely mine. But much of the detail of the narrative is based on a journal I kept during the trip, and some of the text derives from it and from unpublished essays of mine. I shall be interested to see what the critics have to say about the various parts of the job in connection with the oft repeated assumption on their part that they can spot a person's writings anywhere by characteristic tricks of style and thinking.

Most of the critics at the time had never heard of Ricketts, and considered the book something odd. Joseph Henry Jackson, arbiter of the literary tastes of San Francisco, regarded it as suspicious mysticism and refused to grant his imprimatur with a personal Sunday review, but farmed out the narrative half to Scott Newhall to be treated as a yachting book, and had me review the scientific half as a contribution to science (*San Francisco Chronicle*, "This World," December 14, 1941). One of the few reviewers to recognize the book as a collaborative effort and to suggest that it was not always clear who wrote which part, was Donald Culross Peattie (*Saturday Review,* December 27, 1941).[10] As might be expected from the St. Francis of afternoon lawn parties, there were some fatuous statements, such as that of surprise to learn that Ricketts drank beer or indulged in speculations about aphrodisiacs, but he was remarkably close to the mark in this:

> The two utterly disparate sections of the book are not assigned to separate authorship. The title page claims shared collaboration. I find nothing inconceivable about an artist taking a distinct interest in the niceties of systematic zoology; not every scientist is foe to beauty, censor of nonsense, chaste in all his thoughts, and sober on both sides.
>
> There can't be a doubt, for instance, that Ricketts has opened Steinbeck's eyes to the rewards and delights of natural history, or that he has earnestly and meticulously coached him in scientific thought-habits and viewpoints. He has given his ebullient friend a biological philosophy. . . . Mr. Steinbeck

---

[10] Steinbeck did not think much of this review by Peattie, and wrote on a copy sent to Ricketts: "This is the review of a completely humorless man and moreover something of a prig. J. S.   P. S.   And something of a bitch."

One of the frostiest reviews was by my old friend John Lyman in *The American Neptune,* (April 1942), 183. It is still essentially correct (except that as a catalogue of species the book is indispensable), and I was reminded of it by finding that my reference to it was noted by Ed on the flyleaf of his notebook new series #3. I suspect the review may have had some influence on his obvious digging into these matters more seriously in preparation for the plankton chapter and Queen Charlottes book:

> If, then, as an account of a sea voyage, there is little of interest in the book to the nautical historian, its scientific shortcomings are even greater. The authors' purpose, so they tell us in their introduction, 'was to observe the distribution of invertebrates, to see and record their kinds and numbers, how they lived together, what they ate, and how they reproduced.' In this respect they have notably failed. Marine organisms are inextricably bound up with the chemical and physical characteristics of the sea water in which they live. Practically all of them spend their youth as microscopic plankton, drifting with the currents to a favorable spot or being eaten by something larger before only the bare lists of forms taken at each collecting station; and although a great deal of emphasis is laid on the Panamic character of the fauna of the region we are left almost completely in the dark as to why one region should be any different from others in the first place.

appears to have discovered it only yesterday, in its full implications and deep perspectives. . . .

Ed obviously expected this collaboration to go on. During the first year of the war, however, he spent considerable time reading the reports of Japanese scientists on the Pacific islands, and many pages in one of his notebooks are given over to notes on this reading. He presented himself to various intelligence officers in September of 1942 as a research biologist familiar with the scientific literature that could be relevant to the war effort. He gave John Steinbeck and W. K. Fisher as references. Nothing came of it, and in October he was drafted. He was assigned to duty nearby, however. In 1943 Steinbeck went east to New York and *Cannery Row* was published at the end of 1944 (officially 1945). After that, and the end of the war, more people came around and Ed had less time of his own, but he was always looking forward to things that he and Steinbeck would do together—a high school biology textbook for which he wrote an introduction, collecting trips, and perhaps an expedition to South America or to coral reefs. The laboratory business dwindled to almost nothing and Ed worked for California Packing as a lab technician, with time off for collecting trips now and then.

During 1945 and 1946 Ricketts was negotiating seriously with Stanford University on a proposition to build a new laboratory for his activities on the grounds of Hopkins Marine Station, primarily from proceeds to be realized from the sale of the industrial property on Cannery Row, with John Steinbeck as a silent partner. "We have in mind a combination establishment, research, residence, biological supply house, which shall serve as headquarters for our explorations and investigations into the fauna of the Pacific during the next twenty years or so (I am 47, John a few years younger)." (EFR to Lawrence Blinks, Nov. 11, 1944.) Detailed plans were drawn up for this building in 1945, and the lawyers for Stanford University drew up a formal agreement. All the property to be built and installed on the grounds of Hopkins Marine Station was to revert to Stanford University "at our deaths." This matter was discussed with additional plans in November of 1946. However, the decline of the sardines had set in and the property on Cannery Row no longer was of interest to the packing company, and the negotiations were abandoned.

The publication of *Cannery Row*, as Ricketts expected, made him a public personality and attracted interest to the Row and its ways. He thought it "very funny, exceedingly funny, sort of Tortilla Flatish but has a better architecture and an undertone of sadness and lonliness. . . . Because I occurred in it so obviously and so frequently Jn wanted me to OK it, and tho it makes me out to a very romantic figure and I'll practically have to leave town after publication until things quiet down. Still it's a fine job and I approved thoroly." (EFR to EFR Jr., Oct. 23, 1944.) In later letters he commented that the notoriety had not been as great as expected (this was before the end of the war, however). More than a year after the publication of *Cannery Row* a soldier appeared at the door to ask if Ed "was the guy who liked Gregorian music" and volunteered his services as leader of a singing group, and so a pre-Bach singing group was organized and flourished for a while.

An entry in his notebook titled "Program 3-16-46" indicates that Ed was concerned about the time that his life as a celebrity as Doc of *Cannery Row* was costing him (many people had taken to calling on him and he was being "collected" by tourists and students alike). In what is essentially a budget proposal for his time he advises himself to "be affable but not voluble, perfectly civil and friendly, let there be whatever warmth there is but make no specific attempt to convey it" and to take "not more than one or two drinks in an afternoon or during an evening . . . If I want it I'll take it, otherwise not for social pressure unless fairly important." He also proposed to limit himself to "intercourse not oftener than twice a week" and hoped his income would enable him to undergo psychiatry the following year. (Possibly this was something Ed anticipated as an interesting experience in examining his own thought processes rather than a feeling that he might need "head shrinking.")

Sometime in 1946 he began to generate plans for the third part of his project, a work on the fauna of the Queen Charlotte Islands. This work would be part of a trilogy of manuals about the life of Pacific shores—*Between Pacific Tides, Sea of Cortez,* and *The Outer Shores.* They would all be interlocked by cross references and all of them would be revised and kept up to date. He spent a great deal of time designing the various kinds of cards for notes and references—two colors of large 5 x 8 cards and several kinds and colors of 3 x 5's. But this would require several collecting trips to the Queen Charlottes. Ed believed that their geographical situation provided some interesting peculiarities and that there he could learn some things about the evolution of aggregations.

In 1947 Ed applied for a fellowship from the Guggenheim Foundation to support two summer trips to the Queen Charlottes, and possibly the Aleutians. His application was supported by a letter from John Steinbeck. He did not get it. The usual pattern of fellowship was for a year, and the two summers may have disturbed the committee. I once heard, from someone I now cannot recall, that the committee had read *Cannery Row* and *Sea of Cortez* and had visions of a wake of beer cans labeled "Guggenheim" between Monterey and Canada. Apocryphal, no doubt. Perhaps, had Steinbeck made it plain that he planned to go on the trips, Ed might have had better luck. Anyhow, they planned to go together and early in 1948 were making definite arrangements for the expedition.

In the meanwhile, *Between Pacific Tides* dragged on at the Stanford Press, and in a moment of exasperation John Steinbeck and Edward F. Ricketts wrote a "slightly drunken" (E.F.R. to J.W.H., Feb. 17, 1948) letter to the Stanford Press, reproduced in this volume with some in-house jibes scrawled on it. This appears to be their only joint letter, and aside from its quasi-serious mood, suggests that subsequent editions of *Between*

Pacific Tides might have been by Ricketts and Steinbeck (he did prepare a short foreword for the second edition). *The Outer Shores* was planned as a joint operation, like *Sea of Cortez*. But all this was not to be. A week after returning proofs on May 3, 1948, for the revised edition of *Between Pacific Tides* to the Stanford Press, Ed Ricketts was dead.

III

When Ed Ricketts died on May 11, 1948, Steinbeck was at first distraught—he wanted to burn the town down because he had not arrived in time. Nevertheless, he lost no time in removing Ed's safe from the lab and took custody of Ed's journals when it was finally opened. The Stanford Press approached him about the possibility of completing *The Outer Shores* (evidently the Press had already expressed an interest in this work), but he could promise no more than attempt to edit the notes (which was never done). He did write that he intended to edit Ed's journals, but he would not estimate the time it might take. The Stanford Press was obviously interested, as indicated by Steinbeck's letter of July 3, 1948, to Floris P. Hartog of Stanford University Press:

> I have your letter of May 26 for which thank you. It will be a very long time I am afraid before I can get to work on Ed's Journals. Indeed I should like to leave them for some future leisure when I can go over them in quiet and also when some time will have given me more perspective than I now have. I think these journals will prove to be almost the clinical development of the best mind I have ever known. It was a mind that knew itself and yet was apart from itself. Its observations of its own times and of the events that went on about it will be of value I am sure. But that is something I am not going into in a hurry.
>
> You may be sure that when it is done, Stanford Press will surely have a look at it. Always, you must remember though, this mind took in all things and took them in order of their importance. Thus sexual development both in thought and in practice will have a part in direct relation to their actual importance to the human organism.

I look forward in the not too distant future, to going back to Pacific Grove and sitting quietly and going over these journals, commenting where necessary biographically or perhaps critically. Ed's mind had no reticences from itself. It was extremely healthy in that respect and yet it was the most complicated affair. In a great many ways I understood it and I am sure (as must be with all associations) in many ways I did not. But all that is for the future. Be sure only that when it is done, you will have a first refusal of the material. It might be a little too strong meat for the average University Press. We will see whether it is for Stanford.

A sort of querulous bracket and interrogation mark has been entered on this letter beside the remark about sexual development; perhaps it is just as well that Stanford Press was not given first refusal. One difficulty with Ed's personal papers is that quite a few of the people mentioned by name are still alive, twenty-two years later. From what I have seen there is nothing malicious or mean, just sometimes over explicit.

In *The Wide World of John Steinbeck* Peter Lisca suggests that had Ricketts lived, John Steinbeck would have become more involved with the affairs of the Pacific Biological Laboratories and might perhaps have settled down to a quieter kind of life. Certainly his literary output would have been different. It is difficult to think of Ed encouraging John to publish some of his later efforts had he seen them in manuscript; perhaps, with the ever-present stimulation of conversations and doing things with Ed as well as being on his native heath, he would never even have attempted some of those books, or they would have been very different. Ed's sister Frances remembers that while Steinbeck tended to have a possessive interest in what his friend was interested in and perhaps confuse it with his own, Ed was never concerned about such matters and was always willing to share freely with John. "Ed would be troubled with John when he let—not best writing be published because he felt that his best writing was so fine. This is the only way that I ever saw Ed being possessive with John. Ed was sure—long before it was awarded that John would receive the Nobel." (F.S. to J.W.H.,

May 3, 1970.) Concerning the Nobel Prize, incidentally, Steinbeck wrote to me, "Wouldn't Ed have laughed? And we would have drunk gallons of beer." (J.S. to J.W.H., Nov. 1, 1962.) I suppose so, but it would have been gentle, appreciative laughter. Perhaps Steinbeck said something more, somewhere else, that would reveal his indebtedness to his friend. In a letter to Steinbeck sometime in August 1946, just after the death of Ed's mother, Ed wrote: "It's funny that your book will get into me though I don't know it; my nostalgias second hand into you."

It seems obvious to me that Ed was hoping that John would help him with future editions of *Between Pacific Tides;* the preface he had John write for the second edition may have been the opening wedge. They certainly would have collaborated on a book about the Queen Charlottes (perhaps the essay on poetry would have found its way into that one—and I must admit that I do not share Ed's taste for "Black Marigolds"). The idea of a joint work on biology for beginners or high school students may have been mostly Ed's private dream although he did mention it to me (I think again in 1945) and one of his notebook entries has this characteristic self cross reference: "See my introd. for Jn & my biol. text book." So an introduction had been written, but it is not clear whether this is the same as the 1940 draft or was something else (this entry seems to have been made in January 1948). Ed thought that Steinbeck would have been a good biologist, especially with his sharp eyes for details, and was evidently trying to encourage him to be one, or at least join him.

Where would the philosophy have gone? In what direction was Ed going? Certainly he would never have lost his interest in animals, "The good, kind, sane little animals" as he wrote on the flyleaf of one of his notebooks (yet he was not the sort who acquired pets), or the interactions of nature, and he was planning not only the expedition to the Queen Charlottes, but trips out to the desert to examine further the thoughts he had had when driving back from Las Vegas after being married there January 2, 1948 (so his notebook says; the news account of his death states he was married in Paso Robles in April). These thoughts concerned the "high tension thing and its relation to human ecology" which were evidently set in motion by the sight of the huge power lines, "the anastomosing transmission of power from Boulder Dam to Priest Valley & to Monterey penin." He was beginning to think of vectors and tensors involving the strength of the line of relationships between animals, food, energy, and associations, "all this taking place in a large pattern of increasing entropy." Thus, despite his failure with the plankton essay, which must be attributed to the poor "state of the art" at the time, Ed Ricketts obviously would have been in step with current thinking about ecology and might well have contributed some new and useful ideas for this era of human ecology.

In his philosophy, Ed was obviously seeking a "holistic" blend of his diverse reading and thinking, that would lead to a "breaking through" into a more peaceful and positively acquiescent perception of the nature of things. Among his sources were C. G. Jung, whose writings he abstracted in some detail, the Tao, Conrad, Whitman, and Robinson Jeffers. He had a particular fondness for mystics and read Plotinus, Jacob Boehme, and Novalis. He set great store by his philosophical essays and hoped someday to publish them, perhaps under the title "Participation" which he considered "the most deeply interesting thing in the world." Sometime when he became well known through his association with Steinbeck, he thought, the essays might be acceptable to a publisher. His eclectic blend, salted with a dash of Zen, would have been in key with the mood of our times, but obviously the editors of *Harper's* and *Atlantic* were not ready for it in the 1940's.

As for the current concern over the environment and man's future stewardship of it, the concern for wasteful over-exploitation of fisheries resources in the Gulf of California, expressed in *Sea of Cortez,* is familiar to many, and had no small influence on my own way of thinking:

> We liked the people on this boat very much. They were
> good men, but they were caught in a large destructive machine,

good men doing a bad thing. With their many and large boats, with their industry and efficiency, but most of all with their intense energy, these Japanese will obviously soon clean out the shrimps of the region. And it is not true that a species thus attacked comes back. The disturbed balance often gives a new species ascendancy and destroys forever the old relationship.

In addition to the shrimps, these boats kill and waste many hundreds of tons of fish every day, a great deal of which is sorely needed for food. Perhaps the Ministry of Marine had not realized at that time that one of the good and strong food resources of Mexico was being depleted. If it has not already been done, catch limits should be imposed, and it should not be permitted that the region be so intensely combed. Among other things, the careful study of this area should be undertaken so that its potential could be understood and the catch maintained in balance with the supply. Then there might be shrimps available indefinitely. If this is not done, a very short time will see the end of the shrimp industry in Mexico.

We in the United States have done so much to destroy our own resources, our timber, our land, our fishes, that we should be taken as a horrible example and our methods avoided by any government and people enlightened enough to envision a continuing economy. With our own resources we have been prodigal, and our country will not soon lose the scars of our grasping stupidity. But here, with the shrimp industry, we see a conflict of nations, of ideologies, and of organisms. The units of the organisms are good people. Perhaps we might find a parallel in a moving-picture company such as Metro-Goldwyn-Mayer. The units are superb—great craftsmen, fine directors, the best actors in the profession —and yet due to some overlying expediency, some impure or decaying quality, the product of these good units is sometimes vicious, sometimes stupid, sometimes inept, and never as good as the men who make it. The Mexican official and the Japanese captain were both good men, but by their association in a project directed honestly or dishonestly by forces behind and above them, they were committing a true crime against nature and against the immediate welfare of Mexico and the eventual welfare of the whole human species.

It is not difficult to imagine Ed as a fierce partisan of the hearing rooms, where his physical courage or simply lack of concern for physical danger would have enabled him to glare down the Neanderthal types in the big comfortable chairs. (His old collaborator, Jack Calvin, is busy now trying to save some of the last remaining wilderness of coastal Alaska, incidentally.) Perhaps we might by now have had from Steinbeck the great novel of the environmental fight, were they both still with us.

One thing that is difficult to imagine is Ed as an old man of 73; but he looked many years younger than his age, and it seems impossible that he would ever have lost his interest in girls, in finding true relaxation with women, first in bed and then in conversation, in completing good circles of communication and relationship with them (as well as with all other people he met). In one of his notebook entries Ed had a long introversion with himself about the problem of developing ideas with his companion. He had had what he thought was a good idea, but it was squelched: "I felt deflated that it wasn't so consequential after all, that I hadn't in fact discovered anything, just had been feeling inflated, and she took me down, maybe not intending to one bit." So he considered keeping his delicate thoughts to himself—this soliloquy led on to consideration of the difference in another person who was wishy-washy, foolish, and undisciplined, but who would receive his ideas kindly and help him expand. This need for being heard and encouraged, even at the expense of what some might consider inadequate feedback, explains why Ed was sometimes attracted to women his friends found uninteresting. Ed Ricketts was not the first nor will he be the last to confuse the needs of intellect with those of releasing "turgid sacs of sexual products" (a phrase from his essay on the tides).

Eventually, perhaps, Ed might have tried writing about the broader ecological picture, the toto picture, as he would call it, but to do that he would return to certain places where good and interesting thoughts had happened to him. There was a pool in a stream in Priest Valley "above the school" and the "beaver dam below the school" that he listed in his notes along with Blackwell's Corners out in the desert. Among his notes was also some material on "Nostalgia"—all these notes are typed, along with letters to and from Steinbeck (not always dated), and evidently copies had been sent to Steinbeck. Ed once wrote to me that he liked writing that pulled all sorts of things together and one of the last entries in his notebook (other than detailed lists of things to get and pack up for the Queen Charlottes trip) is a curious list of "Greatest extended works—individual" dated February 3, 1948. Since the list is the last indication of Ed's tastes, it seems useful to include it:

1. Esp. contrapunctus No. 19 in Art of the Figure
2. Beethoven Quartette No. 16, Opus 135. The late Beethoven string quartettes
3. Mozart—Don Giovanni
4. Goethe's Faust
5. Joyce Finnegan's Wake

Shorter:
> Black Marigolds
> When lilacs last in the dooryard bloomed
> Out of the cradle endlessly rocking
> Song of the Nightingale

Epics:
> Morte d'Arthur
> Odyssey
> Wm Byrd Mass for 5 voices
> Palestrina Missa Brevis

There are notes following this list about the noble conflict that can't be resolved, as exemplified by Don Giovanni, and the affirmation of Goethe's Faust (the entry concludes with a rough translation of the Chorus Mysticus that ends: Das Ewig-Weibliche/Zieht uns hinan). Off to one side the recorso theme of *Finnegan's Wake* is quoted by copying out the beginning at the end of the book and picking up the opening line, and at the bottom of the page is written: "Humans aren't big enough to bear the vision they conceive."[11]

---

[11] The inclusion of Don Giovanni in the list was because it was his wife's favorite music and he had become interested in it for that reason; as his son remembers, Ed also had, as Steinbeck did, the tendency to identify the interests of others as his own, at least if he loved them.

It is interesting to note that in a way Steinbeck acted out a recorso

In some ways this is a sort of trivial entry, inspired perhaps by reading the long lists in *Finnegan's Wake*. Obviously, however, Ed would have kept on working over ideas, sharing them with people and developing them, perhaps not always from the basis of the great works he listed for that particular day, but some of them he would have kept with him longer than the brief time that was spared to him after writing this "desert island" list. I would hope that his taste for poetry might have become refined; at least T. S. Eliot could have spoken to him, and could have written no more appropriate epitaph than this:

> Old men ought to be explorers
> Here and there does not matter
> We must be still and still moving
> Into another intensity
> For a further union, a deeper communion
> Through the dark cold and the empty desolation,
> The wave cry, the wind cry, the vast waters
> Of the petrel and the porpoise. In my end is my beginning.
>
> (East Coker)

---

theme of his own by returning to New York for his final decline after retreating from his youthful try there so many years before, perhaps "to come to terms with the rabblement for the sake of a little peace and success." (Stanislaus Joyce, *My Brother's Keeper*, Viking, p. 109.) Some interesting parallels between the relationship of the Joyce brothers and of Ricketts and Steinbeck might be developed, especially in light of the statement by Richard Ellman in the introduction: "Inspired cribbing was always part of Joyce's talent; his gift was for transforming material, not for originating it, and Stanislaus was the first of a series of people on whom he leaned for ideas" (p. xv).

The startling contrast between Thomas Mann's story of how he wrote *Dr. Faustus (The Genesis of a Novel)* and Steinbeck's account of the writing of *East of Eden (Journal of a Novel)* suggests that Steinbeck was, even after all his writing, still an amateur man of letters. Of course, *Journal of a Novel* is a posthumous publication, but the care devoted to the journal, including the making of a special box for it, suggests that Steinbeck took it very seriously. But how little it tells us of what really went into the book!

SOURCES

Sources for this account of Ed Ricketts include, in addition to the profile "About Ed Ricketts" by John Steinbeck in *The Log from the Sea of Cortez* and (judiciously) *Cannery Row*, my own notes and letters (correspondence with E. F. Ricketts, 1935-1948), letters from Ricketts' sister, Mrs. Fred Strong of Carmel, correspondence with the Stanford University Press (both my own and letters by Ricketts and Steinbeck in the permanent *Between Pacific Tides* file), and the Ricketts papers at Hopkins Marine Station. These papers include the unpublished manuscript on the tides and a preface to a proposed work on San Francisco Bay life, scraps of notes and professional correspondence (mostly about identifying material for the Sea of Cortez study and the Queen Charlottes). There are also three large page (9¾" x 12") black notebooks with red corners; these are standard faint-lined record books with numbered pages. They are titled as follows: New Series Notebook No. 2, from July 1942 to June 1944 (300 pp); New Series Notebook Number 3, Started Late June 1944, Including Outside Coast Vancouver Island Expedition June July 1945 (150 pp); and NSNB #4 New Series Notebook Number Four, Started Sept. 1945 after first trip to West Coast of Vancouver Island (300 pp., entries end on p. 261 but from p. 297 on there are logistics notes on the proposed trip).

The entries are for the most part in pencil, and are sometimes barely legible. They include notes on collecting localities, reading (the notebooks were taken to libraries and extensive notes on reading were made in libraries wherever Ed happened to be), lists of supplies for trips, and personal entries about ideas, books, projects, and the like. While some of these are of a personal sort one might not expect to find in such a book, mention is made of "formal journals," whose present whereabouts is uncertain. Steinbeck mentions in the profile that he had to remove pages from notebooks because they might embarrass persons before turning them over to Hopkins Marine Station, but only one leaf, pp. 145-46 from book 3 has been removed from these. There are many blank and partially filled pages. The field notes on the Vancouver Island and Queen Charlottes trips were transcribed and occupy seventy-one pages of single-spaced typescript with virtually no margins, in a separate folder.

These three books may have been part of the journals Steinbeck mentions—the last one is closed by Steinbeck, who wrote (with the mistake in the year) on page 261: "E.F.R. was hit by train May 9. died May 11 1947 J.S."

In addition to the above material I have been able to examine, through the courtesy of Peter Lisca, material currently in his possession at

Gainesville, Florida. This includes a large amount of business correspondence, personal correspondence files (including family letters), and the typescript of essays, and notes for several others. Another lot of papers is in the possession of Edward F. Ricketts, Jr. of San Anselmo, California. Although there are scraps and notes of beginnings of several others, only three essays appear to have been finished: "The Philosophy of Breaking Through," "A Spiritual Morphology of Poetry," and "Non-teleological Thinking." There are copies of Ricketts' journal written during the Sea of Cortez trip, his Guggenheim proposal, and a sort of anti-script to *The Forgotten Village*. Copies of much of this material will be placed in the library at Hopkins Marine Station.

Whatever his ultimate intentions were for all this material, Ricketts was obviously a saver and respecter of documents. It is therefore significant that the papers do not include (except for accidental scraps) any correspondence between Ricketts and Steinbeck, and one is regretfully forced to conclude that Steinbeck disposed of some significant material.

APPENDIX

1. A bibliographic summary of *Between Pacific Tides*.

Although the current (1968) edition of *Between Pacific Tides* is officially the fourth edition, it is actually the fifth. James Trosper, of the Stanford University Press, has kindly supplied some of the publishing information included in this summary.

APRIL 1939. First edition. 1000 copies (out of print, 1942-1948). *Between Pacific Tides*. By Edward F. Ricketts and Jack Calvin. An account of the habits and habitats of some five hundred of the common, conspicuous seashore invertebrates of the Pacific Coast between Sitka, Alaska, and northern Mexico.
1939. Stanford University Press, Stanford University, California. London: Humphrey Milford :: Oxford University Press.
xxii + 320 pp, 112 figs., XLVI pls.

AUGUST 1948. Revised edition. 3500 copies. *Between Pacicfic Tides*. An account of the habits and habitats of some five hundred of the common, conspicuous seashore invertebrates of the Pacific Coast between Sitka, Alaska, and northern Mexico. By Edward F. Ricketts and Jack Calvin. Foreword by John Steinbeck. Drawings by Ritchie Lovejoy.
Stanford University Press: Stanford, California :: London: Geoffrey Cumberledge: Oxford University Press. 1948. xxviii + 365 pp, 129 figs., XLVI pls., col. frspce.
The added material is principally the plankton chapter (pages 253-288, figs. 113-129), the foreword by Steinbeck, and the color frontispiece of chitons on a green background. In the preface dated April 1948, signed by E.F.R. and J.C., it is stated that this is considered an "amended edition" and that "Changes involving extension of range, disputed spellings, ambiguities of style, questions of

policy, and revision of the index to include page numbers, purposely have been reserved for a more extended revision."

The Stanford Press added a note dated June 8, 1948 on page x concerning the death of Edward F. Ricketts "on May 12" which states that he had read page proofs and prepared index copy.

SEPTEMBER 1952.   Third edition. 12,500 copies (in 3 printings). Edward F. Ricketts and Jack Calvin. *Between Pacific Tides*. An account of the habits and habitats of some five hundred of the common, conspicuous seashore invertebrates of the Pacific Coast between Sitka, Alaska, and northern Mexico.

Third edition. Revised by Joel W. Hedgpeth. Foreword by John Steinbeck. Line drawings by Ritchie Lovejoy.

Stanford University Press. Stanford, California. 1952. xiii + 502 pp. 134 figs., XLVI pls., col. frspce. Endpaper map.

In this edition a preface "About this book and Ed Ricketts" was written by myself and Jack Calvin (whom I did not meet until April 6, 1970); the long lists of illustrations were removed to make room for this addition to the fore matter. Illustrations, mostly photographs of characteristic environments, were added to the front and back pages of the illustration sections. An addition was added to the plankton chapter, as indicated by brackets, on pp. 371-372. A new chapter, VI, Intertidal Zonation and Related Matters," was added (pp. 375-401). The Appendix was revised completely and the separate reference list for the original plankton chapter was incorporated into it. Endpapers, drawn by me, were added. Except for some easily corrected mistakes (original pagination of the text had to be retained), the text was substantially the same as the second edition up to page 375. Blank space on pages 315-316 was utilized for an insert about Tomales Bay (with a map).

JULY 1962.   Third edition, revised. 17,500 copies (in 5 printings). Edward F. Ricketts and Jack Calvin. *Between Pacific Tides*. An account of the habits and habitats of some five hundred of the common, conspicuous seashore invertebrates of the Pacific Coast between Sitka, Alaska, and northern Mexico.

Third edition, revised. Revisions by Joel W. Hedgpeth. Foreword by John Steinbeck. Line drawings by Ritchie Lovejoy.

Stanford University Press. Stanford, California. 1962. xiii + 516 pp., 135 figs., XLVI pls., col. frspce.

A note was added, ten years later, to the preface about Ricketts, some illustrations were changed, and the plankton chapter was removed, and replaced by a chapter based on recent oceanographic work. Except for some original annotations in the appendix (which are still held to the fourth edition) I am responsible for pages 345—to the end. The Tomales Bay addendum on pages 315-316 was completely rewritten.

OCTOBER 1968.   Fourth edition. 12,000 copies (in 2 printings). Edward F. Ricketts and Jack Calvin. *Between Pacific Tides*.

Fourth edition. Revised by Joel W. Hedgpeth. 1968. Stanford University Press, Stanford, California. xiv + 614 pp., 302 figs., 8 col. pls.

This is the first completely new edition. It has been completely reset; some sections were rearranged, and deletions of out of date material, recognized as such even in 1948, were at last made. I also deleted the foreword by John Steinbeck, partly because about 20% (at least) of the book was no longer the one he wrote about, although I have done my best to carry on in the original style. In previous editions changes could be recognized in the text because they were stripped in on the page masters and came out looking slightly different.

Many illustrations, including some color plates (produced in Japan) were added, and quite a few of the older ones were replaced. All my original diagrams were redrawn, and the endpaper maps incorporated into the text and replaced by one of Nick Carter's photographs.

A completely new preface replaced the former one by myself and Calvin, in part because this has been widely circulated and is still available but more because the record for endurance set by this book called for some words about the genre it represents. I realize that a new public may not have found some of these things as familiar as I did, and some regrets have reached me. But times do change. I do not want to think about what must be done to bring this work completely up to date with all the activity that is now going on along the seashore; it does seem odd to me that no real competition has developed in either the Puget Sound or Southern California areas.

2. A prospectus for *The Outer Shores.*

There are many notes in Ricketts' last notebook concerning this book, and other notes, especially on library reading, which suggest what some of the contents of the book would have been, assuming that Steinbeck would have adopted all of Ricketts' suggestions. The entry on page 224 of NSNB #4 is a tentative outline of the work in progress:

Notes on the next book:

The Outer Shores a record of three summers work in the Queen
    Charlottes & the west coast of Vanc Id.

I.   The West Coast of Vanc Id. prob no pictures
    (a) Clayoquot Sound
    (b) Pt Esteban & other regions.
II. The Queen Charlottes, should be well illustrated with photos,
    perhaps can buy some at Masset & Pr Rupert, but I'll have to
    take most of them
    (a) the Masset region
    (b) Masset Neck
    (c) Skidegate City etc
III. & IV. The Phyletic catalogue
    III.   Introd with statement of methodology
    IV.   Phyletic catalog & Bibliography
             Present set-up   Apr 1948
    (1) John's acct containing among other things a transcript of
my journals for 1945-46 which will include some ideas on

      (a) Ecol. is the science of relationships, vectors

      (b) The species concept doesn't always work for the mar invetebrates

      (c) perhaps some dope from the a/c of the small boat trip to SE Alaska

    (2) List of spp encountered & bibliography incl.

    (3) Introd. to list, which will consider methodology

        (Can get some dope from Guggenheim project in my files) also will compare # of spp encountered per trip with equivalent # Gulf of Calif.

[On opp. page (225) is diagram of various kinds of cards used for the records; evidently an illustration showing the "flow chart" of the card system was intended.]

On page 260 there is a separate outline for the second part (actually Parts III & IV) of the first outline.

Introduct. to the II Part of *The Outer Shores* will include

(a) general statement of the aims of the great programme (this can be got from my Guggenh. statement)

(b) a general statement of the west Vanc id & the QC Ids marine faunas, with comparisons btwn the 2, & btwn each one & other regions also where (as at PG), and with statistics as to the # of spp taken, the # of spp taken, the # taken per tide etc

(c) a statement as to the methodology of the survey in genl.

(d) a key to the concurrent chitons of the whole coast

(e) Perhaps, if I can beast it from him, a key to the Petrolisthes of the N Temp Zone (Cedros Id N) from Steve Glassell

(c) Methodology of the Survey in genl—partic with reference to record keeping (all pioneer work in the past has referred to the worker's memory, now this stuff is being recorded. If you want to check up on Verrill's notes, on his specimens, on anything but his publ work you can't. The background was in his head; & the same seems to be true to a perhaps lesser extent of Dall's ideas, certainly his ideas on zoogeography)

    CONSTRUCT A TABLE OF ORGANIZATION WITH THE VARIOUS PRINTED CARDS AND FORMS IN PLACE and with lines of relationship between them indicated and referring to their documentation. Then have reproductions of the newest editions (after Apr 1948 for the species card, fr inst) of the various printed forms, with positional tabs, & with punch marks in place, all typically filled out.

    Draw one or two graphs of the zoogeogr. summaries, for reproduction as the present graphs of the Brachyura, fr. inst.

    Then give a statement of instructions for filling out the forms & for handling the system, with what practical hints I've been able to work out so far. A statement of how the thing works.

It is obvious from these two outlines and the comments that the book would have been a northern or cold water version of *Sea of Cortez*. Other entries in the notebook indicate that in addition to discussions of vectors in ecology and general problems of speciation there might have been an essay on native life and manners, the present status of the northwest coast Indians (Ricketts read extensively in anthropology, both on the South Seas as well as the Indians of the region and was thinking about the evils done by missionaries and the comparative virtues of the Catholic and Episcopal churches, etc.), and evidently more philosophizing.

ACKNOWLEDGMENTS

We are indebted to Edward F. Ricketts, Jr., Alan Baldridge, Librarian of the Hopkins Marine Station, and Peter Lisca for permission to use quotations from the letters, journals, and papers of Edward F. Ricketts; to Elizabeth Otis for permission to quote unpublished letters of John Steinbeck; and to Rolf L. Bolin, George S. Myers, Sarah Mayea, and others for various suggestions and tidbits of information.

Permission for use of published material has been granted by the Viking Press, Inc. for excerpts from *Cannery Row* by John Steinbeck and *Sea of Cortez* by Steinbeck and Edward F. Ricketts; Stanford University Press for the excerpt from the second edition of *Between Pacific Tides* by Edward F. Ricketts and Jack Calvin; University of Chicago Press for the use of paragraphs from *Animal Aggregations* by W. C. Allee, (copyright 1931); and to Harcourt, Brace and World for use of the excerpt from "East Coker" by T. S. Eliot from *Four Quartets*.

ROBERT M. BENTON

THE ECOLOGICAL NATURE OF *CANNERY ROW*

IT IS UNFORTUNATE that it often takes the death of a writer to encourage the dispassionate evaluation of his work, that which should be the hallmark of literary criticism. The history of letters confirms this fact, and the death of John Steinbeck is a case in point. Throughout the last years of his life, critics spoke of Steinbeck's decline as a writer. In *American Literary Scholarship: An Annual/1965*, C. Hugh Holman, in reviewing Steinbeck scholarship for the year, says, "Clearly Steinbeck, a recent Nobel Prize winner, is receiving serious attention from some of our academic critics, yet much of what they write is defensive or apologetic, as the fine Steinbeck issue of *Modern Fiction Studies* plainly shows." Steinbeck has been acclaimed for *The Grapes of Wrath, East of Eden,* and a few other pieces, but much of his work has been called minor. This has been especially true of *Cannery Row*.

Critical comments about Steinbeck's work have often suggested that *Cannery Row* was an inferior novel. It has been said that the 1954 publication of *Sweet Thursday* impressed most reviewers as a disappointing reversion to the vein of *Tortilla Flat* and *Cannery Row*. *Cannery Row* has been labeled a delightfully inconsequential book. It may be that those who have praised *The Grapes of Wrath* as a powerful social thesis novel have missed the thesis of *Cannery Row*, a thesis which has a particular relevance for the 70's. That thesis is clearly seen in the structure of the novel itself.

Few serious readers of Steinbeck would deny what Frederick Bracher calls the biological cast of Steinbeck's thinking ("Steinbeck and the Biological View of Man," *Steinbeck and His Critics,* p. 183). It is a prominent feature of *The Sea of Cortez* and becomes a major theme in *The Grapes of Wrath.*

> What appears in Steinbeck's novels is . . . a point of view, in the literal sense of that phrase—a way of looking at things characteristic of a biologist. It comprises Steinbeck's typical attitude toward the characters in his novels and also the attitudes of some of the characters themselves. In particular, it appears as the typical values and virtues of Steinbeck's "heroes"—not necessarily the protagonists of the novels, but the characters with whom the reader is obviously intended to sympathize. The manifestations in the novels of this point of view throw light on the development of Steinbeck's thinking, yet, in a welter of comment on Steinbeck's economic, social, moral, and political views, there has been very little mention of this basic attitude toward man (Bracher, p. 184).

Steinbeck, the biologist, is everywhere apparent in his works, and the particular biological cast of his mind is indicated in *The Sea of Cortez.* In specifying his and Ricketts' concern, Steinbeck made the following statement:

> Our own interest lay in relationships of animal to animal. If one observes in this relational sense, it seems apparent that species are only commas in a sentence, that each species is at once the point and the base of a pyramid, that all life is relational to the point where an Einsteinian relativity seems to emerge. And then not only the meaning but the feeling about species grows misty. One merges into another, groups melt into ecological groups until the time when what we know as life meets and enters what we think of as non-life: barnacle and rock, rock and earth, earth and tree, tree and rain and air. And the units nestle into the whole and are inseparable from it. Then one can come back to the microscope and the tide pool and the aquarium. But the little animals are found to be changed, no longer set apart and alone. And it is a strange thing that most of the feeling we call religious, most of the mystical outcrying which is one of the most prized and used and desired reactions of our species, is really the understanding and the attempt to

say that man is related to the whole thing, related inextricably
to all reality, known and unknowable (216-217).

It is Steinbeck the ecologist who wrote *Cannery Row*. It is
then the "ecological" cast of Steinbeck's thinking—that which
causes him to see man as an organism related to a vast and
complex ecosystem—which underlines his novels.

The introductory statement in *Cannery Row* points to the
major conception of the author which controls his handling of
the work:

> Cannery Row in Monterey in California is a poem, a stink,
> a grating noise, a quality of light, a tone, a habit, a nostalgia, a
> dream. Cannery Row is the gathered and scattered, tin and iron
> and rust and splintered wood, chipped pavement and weedy
> lots and junk heaps, sardine canneries of corrugated iron, honky
> tonks, restaurants and whorehouses, and little crowded gro-
> ceries, and laboratories and flophouses. Its inhabitants are, as
> the man once said, "whores, pimps, gamblers, and sons of
> bitches," by which he meant Everybody. Had the man looked
> through another peephole he might have said, "Saints and angels
> and martyrs and holy men," and he would have meant the same
> thing (1).

In the first paragraph of the novel Steinbeck says that
Cannery Row cannot be known and understood apart from the
relationships and interrelationships which exist in it. It is more
than people, than real estate, than buildings. It is all of these,
as they react upon one another, and it is more. It is Mack, Doc,
Lee Chong, the Palace Flophouse, Dora Flood's, Frankie, Joey,
Darling, Old Tennis Shoes, a gopher, and it is more. It is Monterey's attitude toward Josh Billings, Willard's cruelty to Joey,
Doc's love of beer; it is frogs, starfish, abandoned but inhabited
pipes, black stink bugs, and it is more. But it is never less. The
canneries are not Cannery Row; Doc is not; Mack and the boys
are not. They are only a part of that larger living organism, just
as Jim Casy and Tom Joad were parts of another organism.

Several critics have shed light on Steinbeck's achievement
in *Cannery Row*, but seldom has his general pattern been seen.
In attempting to show that *Cannery Row* is in the pastoral tradition, Stanley Alexander suggests that the tide pool is "the

controlling metaphor of the work" ("*Cannery Row:* Steinbeck's Pastoral Poem," *Western American Literature,* II, No. 4 [Winter, 1968], 281-295). Peter Lisca goes even farther when he suggests that "Lee Chong is successful in Cannery Row because he does not fight his environment, but adjusts his business to fit it. . . . In biological terms, Steinbeck might have said that Lee Chong succeeded in converting a parasitic into a commensal relationship" (*The Wide World of John Steinbeck,* pp. 201-202). Lisca mentions a number of commensal relationships in the novel, but he then points to a lack of apparent structure as the greatest difficulty the novel affords. Perhaps the solution to the structural difficulty of the novel can be found in the commensal relationships portrayed when those relationships are seen in connection with the central metaphor of the tide pools and with Steinbeck's acknowledged interest in ecology.

Steinbeck begins his novel with the short descriptive section on Cannery Row. He notes that it is composed of various parts—both human and nonhuman. He shows how Cannery Row comes to life when a catch has been made, and how it settles back into a routine once the "last fish is cleaned and cut and cooked and canned." Then he poses a question: "How can the poem and the stink and the grating noise—the quality of light, the tone, the habit and the dream—be set down alive?" He answers his question by means of an analogy from marine biology—he will open the page and "let the stories crawl in by themselves." A humorous statement? Indeed. But it is more. It is an early clue into the reason for the structure of the story which will follow.

In Chapter One the omniscient author presents Lee Chong, describing his relationship with Horace Abbeville and with Mack and the boys. At least two types of relationships are shown immediately. One is that which exists among Mack and the boys. Mack is described as the "elder, leader, mentor, and to a small extent the exploiter of a little group of men who had in common no families, no money, and no ambitions beyond food, drink, and contentment." Here is a small, self-contained group living a general commensal relationship with one another. But they have relationships which extend beyond their small group. We see the relationship with Lee Chong in connection with their acquiring the Palace Flophouse. We are told that two of the group sometimes collect frogs and cats for Western Biological and that another is a sometime bartender. There is more here, however, than a description of the sort of relationships which inevitably tie together most stories. Steinbeck seems to take great care in showing how the interrelationships are mutually beneficial, and he uses the acquisition of the Palace Flophouse by Mack and the boys as a prime example:

> ' Everyone was happy about it. And if it be thought that Lee Chong suffered a total loss, at least his mind did not work that way. The windows were not broken. Fire did not break out, and while no rent was ever paid, if the tenants ever had any money, and quite often they did have, it never occurred to them to spend it any place except at Lee Chong's grocery (7).

Here Steinbeck has presented the commensal relationship, that of an organism or group of organisms living with, on, or in another, without injury to either.

Not all of the relationships in *Cannery Row* are commensal, but the fact that so many are indicates the pattern of the novel. Steinbeck continues the pattern of relationships with the second chapter. He says that Lee Chong is more than just a Chinese grocer. "He must be. Perhaps he is evil balanced and held suspended by good—an Asiatic planet held to its orbit by the pull of Lao Tze and held away from Lao Tze by the centrifugality of abacus and cash register—Lee Chong suspended, spinning, whirling among groceries and ghosts" (8). But if Lee Chong is an Asiatic planet in the vast universe, so are "Mack and the boys, too, spinning in their orbits" (9). Having quickly established another kind of ecosystem inhabited by his characters, Steinbeck ends the chapter by praying to "Our Father who art in nature."

Chapter Three presents other aspects of Cannery Row. We are shown the whorehouse of Dora Flood with a watchman named Alfred who "has triumphed over his environment and has brought his environment up with him" (10). Dora has learned to live in Cannery Row by being more law-abiding than anyone else, but William, the previous watchman, could not adjust and destroyed himself. Bit by bit, Steinbeck drops the pieces into place and the entire interlocking set of relationships is established. The central figure is Doc and Western Biological. Of all the characters Doc is most fully able to understand his place in the web of life. "Doc tips his hat to dogs as he drives by and the dogs look up and smile at him. He can kill anything for need but he could not even hurt a feeling for pleasure" (16). He is one who "dug himself into Cannery Row" and "was concupiscent as a rabbit and gentle as hell" (17). Doc has been called the "local deity" of Cannery Row (Lisca, 212), and the attempt of the residents of Cannery Row to throw a party for Doc provides the novel its central action.

Once Doc has been presented, Steinbeck uses Chapter Six to describe the ecology of the Great Tide Pool. The activities of the organisms in the tide pool are remarkable, but, as Doc observes, "the really incredibly remarkable thing is that we find it remarkable. We can only use ourselves as yardsticks" (23). The suggestion here is that there are yardsticks other than those man has traditionally used. Man has traditionally seen himself as more than animal, and Steinbeck seems to suggest that man must first understand himself as fully animal. He validates this concept in a letter to the editors of *Steinbeck and His Critics* (307) when he says the following:

> It is interesting to me that so many critics, instead of making observations, are led to bring charges. It is not observed that I find it valid to understand man as an animal before I am prepared to know him as man. It is charged that I have somehow outraged members of my species by considering them part of a species at all.

In viewing man as animal within the web of life, Steinbeck was apparently twenty years ahead of his time. His statement in *The Sea of Cortez*, published in 1941 and quoted earlier in this study, suggests that Steinbeck was concerned with ecological relationships two decades before a similar concern was noted in the writings of eminent biologists. But note current biological thinking. In the "Editor's Foreword" to *The Subversive Science: Essays Toward An Ecology of Man* (New York, 1969), A. Starker Leopold says, "With all his technological miracles, man is still basically an animal, with all the natural needs, reactions, and dependencies of an animal." And in the "Preface" to the same volume, editors Paul Shepard and Daniel McKinley note the following: "To a world which gives grudging admission of the 'nature' in human nature, we say that the framework of human life is all life and that anything adding to its understanding may be ecological." This is Steinbeck's message in *Cannery Row.*

Steinbeck had written to Pascal Covici at the end of 1940 expressing some of his concern for man:

> So we go into this happy new year, knowing that our species has learned nothing, can as a race learn nothing—that the experience of ten thousand years has made no impression on the instincts of the million years that preceded. (Quoted by Peter Lisca in "John Steinbeck: A Literary Biography," *Steinbeck and His Critics,* 13.)

He feared that man, unlike other animals, might not learn from his experiences, and he must have desired to communicate what he believed to be man's proper relationship to his world. Therefore, immediately following the war, Steinbeck wrote *Cannery Row* which would not only talk about the way in which man fits into the web of life, but also be structured in such a way as to demonstrate the essential substance of his belief.

When one reads *Cannery Row,* one must note the developing set of relationships. Although Doc is the central character and the main action of the work concerns him, he is only one element, however major. Chapter Eight, a presentation of Mr. and Mrs. Sam Malloy, is a humorous account of Mrs. Malloy's desire to have curtains for her windowless boiler-home. Apparently it has no connection with the major action of the plot, but the major action of the plot is only a surface covering for a work in which Steinbeck demonstrates wider concerns. To understand the ecology of Cannery Row is to understand people who live in boilers and who need curtains for them. It is also important to understand something about the nature of Monterey, a larger ecosystem, to comprehend that of Cannery Row, a smaller ecosystem existing within the larger. Monterey is a city which could become concerned about the "tripas" of Josh Billings for fear of the city's honor (Chapter Twelve) but did not want Frankie in school (Chapter Ten) and could find "no place for him." Perhaps Monterey is best portrayed as that city whose major interests concern activities such as flagpole skating (Chapter Nineteen) and whose most interesting questions are spoken by the brilliant young man, Richard Frost: "How—how do you —go to the toilet?"

In theme, plot, and structure, Steinbeck the biologist who is primarily concerned with ecological connections is everywhere apparent. He takes the role of teacher, guiding the student to understand the relationship of organisms in an environment and to observe the processes that link organisms and place. In fact, the exact words found in a leading high school biology text could have been said by Steinbeck. *High School Biology: BSCS Green Version* (Chicago, 1963) contains the following statement in a discussion of the necessity for ecological concern:

> Since a community is a web of interactions, it is convenient to begin a description with one species and let its relationships to other species lead us into the community as a whole. . . . Clearly, the study of a community . . . is not an easy kind of research. But without it we can never fully understand the world in which we live, never develop the ecological machinery for voyaging out of this world, never understand any other world on which we might find life (54,56).

Here the high school text presents the rationale behind the structure of *Cannery Row* and then justifies such an approach. Later in the BSCS text the authors assert, "We do not know of any species of organism that exists independently of all other species. And from what we do know of the living world, it seems that such a situation is impossible" (73).

Doc, Steinbeck's spokesman, ends *Cannery Row* reading aloud some lines of poetry. The lines speak of the poet's love of nature—the trees and flowers, mountains and hills, as well as the sea—and he knows that he has "savored the hot taste of life." Then Doc closes the book of verse. "And the white rats scampered and scrambled in their cages. And behind the glass the rattlesnakes lay still and stared into space with their dusty frowning eyes." The journey is sufficiently complete. Steinbeck has given a glimpse of a community. His achievement as a writer and ours as readers will depend upon how well we understand the relationships among all the organisms in the community. And Steinbeck's wish, I would guess, would be that our concept of ourselves might have changed.

CHARLES R. METZGER

STEINBECK'S MEXICAN-AMERICANS

JOHN STEINBECK completed twenty volumes of novels, short stories, plays, motion picture books, and filmscripts during the years 1929 to 1962. Half deal in part or altogether with Mexicans of one sort or another. Of this half only three works treat of native-born Mexicans living *in* Mexico, i.e., *The Forgotten Village, The Pearl,* and *Viva Zapata!* Seven deal with Mexican-Americans, i.e., with Mexican-born immigrants to Upper California, or with California-born natives of Mexican descent.

Steinbeck mentions by name nearly sixty Mexican-American characters in the seven works: *The Pastures of Heaven, To a God Unknown, Tortilla Flat, The Long Valley, Cannery Row, The Wayward Bus,* and *Sweet Thursday.* Granting that it is not possible in a short paper like this to deal specifically with each of Steinbeck's Mexican-American characters, I suggest that it may yet be worthwhile to deal with a lesser number of representative ones. This is what I propose to do.

Although Steinbeck deals significantly with Mexican-American characters in the two earlier works, *The Pastures of Heaven* and *To a God Unknown,* I propose to deal first with those appearing in *Tortilla Flat.* I do so for several reasons. For one thing, a good half of Steinbeck's Mexican-American characters appear in that work. For another, it is, for better or worse, the most widely known of Steinbeck's works dealing with Mexican-American characters. For another and more important reason, Steinbeck, in developing the "tragic-comic" theme which he says pervades the work—in interpreting by indirections each

141

incident included within the work "morally, esthetically, historically, in the manner of the *paisanos* themselves," presents
repeatedly evidence in support of his two main reasons for
liking *paisanos*, i.e., for thinking Mexican-Americans, for thinking possibly any persons, admirable. He finds *paisanos* interesting and admirable by virtue: (1) of their ability to "merge successfully with their habitat," which "ability in men," says Steinbeck, "is called philosophy," and (2) by virtue of their "strong
but different philosophic-moral system," which appears to make
such successful merging possible for these people.

Steinbeck's interest in all people, and in *paisanos* specifically, is in effect both scientific and in a sense romantic. As a
scientist, he identifies his characters, the *paisanos*, biologically,
in terms of structure and habitat, in terms of genetic origin and
range of distribution. To the question, What is a *paisano?* Steinbeck answers:

> He is a mixture of Spanish, Indian, Mexican and assorted
> Caucasian bloods. His ancestors have lived in California for a
> hundred or two years. He speaks English with a paisano accent
> and Spanish with a paisano accent. When questioned concern-
> ing his race, he indignantly claims pure Spanish blood and rolls
> up his sleeve to show that the soft inside of his arm is really
> white. . . . He is a paisano, and he lives in that uphill district
> above the town of Monterey called Tortilla Flat, although it
> isn't flat at all.*

Subsequently in the novel, and somewhat also after the
manner of a biological scientist, Steinbeck describes his *paisanos*
in their relations to local climate, food supply, and, since they
are men, in relation to such modes of shelter, clothing, habits,
and customs as are prevalent in the area over which they range.
For example, the climate around Monterey is mild. Except for
sea-formed fogs and overcasts, it is mostly sunny and arid. One
can easily live in it, as the *paisanos* do when it pleases them,
with a minimum of clothing and shelter. They can sleep, as for
centuries before them their Indian ancestors did, in the woods

---

*Compare with *paisano* as defined in the *Diccionario Mexico Nuevo*,
"Que es del mismo pais, lugar. Campesino. El que no es militar."

or on the beach. They gain their food, as did their Indian ancestors, by a latter-day version of hunting, fishing, gathering, and barter, with minimum recourse to so-called gainful employment and the use of money. They eat what has been traditionally consumed in the area for centuries—beans, tortillas, some vegetables and fruit, some chicken and fish or other meat protein—and they drink the wine of California or anything else they can get hold of.

Historically, as I have suggested, the *paisanos'* mode of subsistence is a venerable and traditional one traceable back through the customs of their Mexican ancestors to the customs of their Indian ancestors, and modified, like all surviving traditional modes, to adjust to current conditions, namely those in and around Monterey just after the end of World War I. Steinbeck's view of the *paisanos* of Tortilla Flat is in effect scientific in a version of the way that Ed Ricketts' view of the cephalopods of Monterey Bay was, that is, both taxonomical and ecological. But with men, even more noticeably than with octopi, ecological study pursued with even minimal industry quickly develops into sociological study of habits, customs, and traditions. And for men, certainly, these are just as much a part of environment as, say, temperature range. It is at this point, upon expanding the study of environment to include habits, customs, and traditions, that we come face to face with "the strong but different philosophic moral system" of Steinbeck's *paisanos*. This "different philosophical moral system" of the *paisanos* operates, Steinbeck suggests, in two ways: negatively or conservatively, by means of a Thoreau-like economy to protect the integrity of the organism as biological man; and positively or liberally, by way of promulgating and sanctioning a romantic image of a life-style for the man conceived as a conscious, self-regulating individual.

Somewhat after the manner of Thoreau at Walden, the *paisanos* live economically, in terms of money and effort, at the subsistence level. They are, as Steinbeck says, "clean of commercialism [and therefore] free from the complicated systems of American business, and, having nothing that can be stolen, exploited or mortgaged, that system has not attacked them vigorously."

They live lives singularly devoid of the imperatives that dominate most of their non-*paisano* neighbors, devoid of the imperatives outlined by the so-called Protestant work-ethic. They do not work in order to avoid idleness or sin. They do not accept the concept of sin as a chastening and regulating instrument. Rather they look upon the sinful act (for example Big Joe's stealing four of the Pirate's "two-bitses") as an unfortunate human fact to be punished or forgiven as each act warrants. They do not work to gain or defend the status, the approval, the luxury, that derive from traditionally symbolized wealth. Yet they are not altogether opposed to work. Danny has a trade, he is a mule-skinner; the Pirate is a woodchopper; Tall Bob Smoke is a somewhat inept dog catcher. Tito Ralph spends most of his time in jail serving in the official capacity of jailer.

When there is a big party coming up, the *paisanos* are willing to work for as much as a whole day to get money for the party, when, of course, there is no other way to get it. Even the salvaging of lost articles of property to get money, articles such as a skiff, a water-soaked copy of Bowditch, a gallon of wine, or a sack of dried beans for immediate use, requires some effort, particularly when, in the case of the wine or the beans, it is necessary to arrange for the article to get lost in the first place.

The *paisanos* have not, of course, taken even the initial step in the direction of arriving at the more sophisticated work-esthetic understood by such Steinbeck characters as Juan Chicoy, Joseph and Mary Rivas, and their Anglo counterpart, Doc. Their economy is the more exclusively negative, the more practically defensive economy of an ancient citizenry that has been invaded, surrounded, and outnumbered by newer neighbors subscribing to a foreign ethic. As Steinbeck suggests, "the old inhabitants of Monterey" have, like the "Ancient Britons . . . embattled in Wales" survived and indeed prevailed by refusing to change in crucial ways. They have refused to give up the less strenuous ways of living practiced by their Indian and Mexican campesino ancestors. They have refused to accept the gross forms of ambition, of materialism, of pride and guilt imported by their new and unsought neighbors—except, of course, on those rare occasions when to do so is consistent with their pre-existent life style, as in the case of Peaches Ramirez's joining the Native Daughters of the Golden West.

Steinbeck's *paisanos* have refused to subscribe to those views of the world and of right conduct in it which would render them respectable and/or understandable to such neighbors or readers as have bought the White Anglo-Saxon Protestant ethic. They have refused essentially by way of defending their own positive, more liberal, more nearly aristocratic, because romantic in the old sense, image of an appropriate life style. It was not at all by accident or in the interest of irony that Steinbeck chose to describe his *paisanos* in Arthurian terms—after the manner of that great and wistful romantic Thomas Mallory who celebrated the ancient, embattled, and romantic Britons, the knights of the round table, in his own prose.

Perhaps before discussing the knightly virtues ascribed to Danny and demonstrated by him and his *paisano* friends, I ought to say a few words about their romantic self-deceptions, i.e., their lying in order to justify, among other things, their thievery. In its own special way the lie, the romantic deception, is a necessary as well as a satisfactory instrument for making realistic adjustments to the romantic's idealistic image of exemplary conduct. I am suggesting in effect that every romantic, if he is to make his romanticism work, must of necessity operate on occasion after the realistic manner of the picaro. Thus, out of Big Joe's solicitous concern for the welfare of one of Mrs. Morales' chickens, develops a badly needed chicken dinner. Out of a shortage of chickens and a ready supply of sea gulls develop some of Mrs. Pastanos' memorable tamales. Without an instrument of rationalization, without romantic deception, these necessary practical adjustments to reality would have been impossible to achieve gracefully, while yet maintaining the romantic image of a properly mannered and adventurous life style. Possibly Steinbeck had the romantic's need for adjustment to some of the grimmer aspects of reality in mind when he said of the "Arthurian Cycle," what he could have said of his *paisano* cycle, that the stories contain "the stuff psychiatry is made of," the stuff, the rationale, of the psychology of adjustment.

To the charge, often made, that Steinbeck's treatment of his *paisanos* is romantic and sentimental, I can only answer that: (a) it most certainly *is* romantic, and (b) that such romanticism *is not* sentimental, but rather appropriate—that it actually fits the facts of life as life was conducted by the kinds of real persons who provided Steinbeck with models for his fictional characters. Steinbeck of course makes these two assertions himself practically outright by pointedly directing his readers' attention to the Arthurian analogues by means of which he develops his narrative. That such analogues puzzle some readers is due in part to the fact that they, not Steinbeck, are perhaps excessively literal minded. But it may be due in part also to the fact that Steinbeck does not specifically tell his Anglo readers what he knows, and what most Mexican-Americans know, about the very real and actively operating conceptions of the "dignidad de la persona," of being "muy hombre," of being "macho." These conceptions describe in Mexican terms some of the very real things that Steinbeck is talking about when he refers to the *paisanos'* "different philosophic moral system," when, indeed, he describes his *paisanos,* as seen through their own eyes, in aristocratic Arthurian terms.

The phrase "dignidad de la persona" as demonstrated by Steinbeck's *paisanos* does not involve the braggadocio of the *macho* (the self love, for example, of Katherine Anne Porter's obese Braggioni in *Flowering Judas*), does not suggest that which Braggioni stands for, the boastfulness of the *valentón* who brags about his masculine beauty, his bigotes, his size, his courage, so much as it suggests that dignity, quiet or boisterous, which is born of respect for the man as a steadfastly self-determining, self-regulating individual—whether he be *paisano* or knight errant, whether he be drunk or sober, in jail or outside it—so long as he has achieved what Whitman referred to as an awareness of the identified self. Indeed there are few if any *valentóns* in Steinbeck's fiction, none of that unsavory sort captured by Miss Porter in her portrayal of Braggioni, or by Hemingway in his portrait of the wounded Italian officer hero in *A Farewell to Arms*. I suspect, in this connection, that Steinbeck is not so much concerned by his omission with denying the fact that *valentóns* exist, so much as he is with celebrating the dignity of a superior sort of romantic hero, one more like Danny, one possessing in vernacular form a dignity akin to that of Chaucer's knight, the dignity of one who exhibits the "courtesy beyond politeness" of the *paisano*, the courtesy which Chaucer called *gentilesse*.

Indeed Steinbeck's *paisanos* are not soldiers any longer. It is no accident that *paisano* in Mexican-Spanish refers, among other things, to "el que no es militar." Like Hemingway's heroes in *The Sun Also Rises*, the *paisanos* are discharged veterans of World War I. They, like Hemingway's veterans, are not professional soldiers after the manner of Scott Fitzgerald's Tommy Barban in *Tender is the Night*. Rather more like Hemingway's veterans, Steinbeck's *paisanos* are civilian, picaresque heroes-of-the-night, and such fighting as they do is unorganized, unpremeditated, and mainly recreational.

Although they respect a man, and measure him, in terms of his willingness to fight and his relative success at it, their concern is more with those branches of chivalric endeavor having to do with errant adventure and courtly love. In this respect they are again very much like Hemingway's veterans in *The Sun Also Rises*, with this distinctive difference—they are more generous. They share their women, politely, without rancor, each graciously observing accustomed propriety, each courteously waiting his turn, or perhaps his chance. Teresina Cortez, accordingly, does not, frankly, know which of Danny's friends is responsible for her current conditions. As amorists the *paisanos* not only do not compete viciously, as Robert Cohn and

Mike Campbell do for Lady Brett, they look after each other's interests. Pilon and Pablo are concerned that Danny might be lured into matrimony by Mrs. Morales. Danny and the others lend the Pirate the best items of their only clothing so that he can appear dressed properly at the dedication of his gold candlestick to San Francisco de Assisi in the Church of San Carlos in Monterey. They manage to keep Mr. Torrelli from claiming ownership of Danny's remaining house. They share housing, food, and wine, as well as women. As amorists the *paisanos,* after the manner of courtly Arthurians, perform love service. Jesus Maria Corcoran plans to give Arabella Gross a pink rayon brassiere. Rebuffed by her and her soldier companions, he allows Danny to give it to Mrs. Morales. Danny gives a motorless "sweeping machine" to Sweets Ramirez. He, like his friends, grants favors to ladies upon request, or when they do not object too vigorously.

As befits their nobility, their courtesy beyond politeness, the *paisanos* perform genuinely good deeds on behalf of the Pirate, of the Caporal with the infant son, on behalf of Teresina Cortez and her many hungry children. They even, on occasion, round up dogs for Tall Bob Smoke by way of protecting him in his office of dog catcher, being careful to return borrowed pets to the neighborhoods of their masters after their capture has been recorded.

Like Galahad the *paisanos* seek, but do not quite find, a version of the Holy Grail. And they are at least religiously proper, when not truly devout. Much, for example, as Danny's friends are pained by their propriety, they refrain from attending his funeral mass because they can not be properly dressed. They respect the piety of others—of the Pirate, of Cornelia Ruiz, of Teresina's aged mother Angelica Cortez. They honor the memory of their heroic dead, of Arthur Morales "dead in France . . . for his country."

Danny, of course, is chief of the *paisano* heroes. After his passing, as after the passing of King Arthur, the group dissolves. The hero cannot be replaced. Of Danny deceased the group agrees in summary that "that Danny who had fought for lost causes, or any other kind; that Danny who could drink glass for glass with any man in the world; that Danny who responded to the look of love like an aroused tiger," that "*that* Danny was a man for you!"—that Danny was "muy hombre," exemplary in "his goodness, his courage, his piety."

One can argue with some justice that the knights of the round table were not so alcoholic as Danny and his friends, that Steinbeck has romanticized alcoholism and understated its degenerative and lethal effect. Yet the fact remains that Danny's heroic passing is occasioned by alcohol. And the reader must bear also in mind that Steinbeck is telling his story in "the manner of the *paisanos* themselves." And it turns out that the *paisanos* are relatively undeceived. They are aware that "there are plenty of people who die through abuse of wine." They are aware, or at least Steinbeck's readers are made aware, of the depressive, of the often violently manic, as well as the sociable effects of drink.

One also can argue with strong justification that Steinbeck's presentation of his *paisanos* does not do anything like justice in the way of presenting the very powerful family ties that dominate the lives of most Mexican-Americans. But not all persons classed in any type can be guaranteed, or even realistically expected, to fit into all the sub-categories of the type. Strong family ties, as a matter of fact, do not show up much in Mallory either. Indeed, whether in literature or in real life, romantic-chivalric heroes tend in the main not to be family men, at least not while they are romantic and chivalrous.

It is necessary now, at last, to point out that Steinbeck's portrayal of *paisanos* in *Tortilla Flat* does not purport to do more than present one kind of Mexican-American, the *paisano* errant, in one place, Monterey, and at one time, just after World War I.

Not all of Steinbeck's Mexican-American characters adjust to the environment of Monterey County, particularly to its changing social environment, as successfully as the *paisanos*. In

The Pastures of Heaven, for example, all five of the Mexican-Americans either referred to or portrayed by Steinbeck run into one form or another of tragic or near tragic difficulty. The Spanish Corporal who around 1776 stumbled across and named Las Pasturas del Cielo subsequently died of the pox contracted from an Indian woman. The real-life nineteenth century bandit Tiburcio Vasquez, romanticized by Molly Morgan, died a *bandido-macho's* early, violent death. The idiot-savant Tularecito is sent to the asylum for the criminally insane at Napa as a direct consequence of his forced exposure to elementary education. The pious Lopez sisters who manage to make their restaurant pay by "giving themselves" to all customers who eat three or more enchiladas are forced by a jealous wife to abandon their business and go to San Francisco to become "bad women" and to take the money of shame.

Pepe Torres in the "Flight" portion of *The Long Valley* is tricked by the combination of his innocent conception of masculine pride and the archaic revenge code still practiced in California into becoming "a man" too soon, hustled into death before he has had a fair chance to achieve, much less to enjoy, functional manhood. The Gitano in "The Great Mountains" section of *The Red Pony* does manage to retain even in death his "dignidad de la persona" against the taunts of Carl Tiflin, a dignity, incidentally, counterpart to that of "Grandfather," the anachronistic "Leader of the People." This use of Mexican-American and Anglo counterparts by Steinbeck is not unique to *The Red Pony.* Versions of it show up also in *To a God Unknown, The Wayward Bus,* and *Sweet Thursday.*

In these three works Steinbeck treats of Mexican-American characters who adjust to their environment more successfully even than Steinbeck's *paisanos.* And the Mexican-American characters paired with similar or contrasting Anglo characters appear to adjust to their changing environment at least as well as the Anglos. In setting up these pairs of characters, Joseph Wayne and Juanito in *To a God Unknown,* Juan Chicoy and Pimples Carson in *The Wayward Bus,* Joseph and Mary Rivas and Doc in *Sweet Thursday,* Steinbeck has done something that structurally is very important. He has set up comparisons that enable us to see that for Steinbeck both the concept of the "dignidad de la persona," and the matter of being "muy hombre," are important to him not only as instruments of human adjustment to environment but also as measures for judging men, Anglos as well as Mexican-Americans.

Although Steinbeck introduces about twelve important and interesting Mexican-American characters in *To a God Unknown,* characters such as old Juan and his guitar playing son-in-law, such as Willie Romas and his father the drover, such as the Garcia family, the most important Mexican-American character is Juanito, who is paired with his friend Joseph Wayne. The two friends work Joseph's cattle ranch together during the period preceding World War I. They marry at about the same time, become fathers about the same time. They are both religious syncretists, mixing ancient and animistic religious feelings with elements selected from conventional piety. Both risk death in cause of conscience. But Juanito survives, whereas Joseph dies sacrificially.

Significantly, Juanito, who begins the story as subordinate, as assistant to Joseph, learns enough by the end of the novel to say to his friend, "There are things you do not know"—things which presumably Juanito knows, and which Father Angelo also knows. Like Steinbeck's *paisanos* Juanito is part Indian, yet claims pure Castilian blood. Like them he subscribes to a medieval code of honor, in his case to the revenge code. Having slain Joseph's brother Benjy in the act of seducing his wife, Juanito then requests that Joseph kill him by way of avenging Benjy's murder. The request rejected, Juanito exiles himself, returning after a proper time to confess to Father Angelo and to try to help his friend. For Juanito the sentiments of friendship, piety, honor, love of family, and respect for time-honored mores direct his life. He is not "macho," but rather quietly "muy hombre," and he prevails by virtue of his resolute observance of the dictates of his Indian-Spanish heritage, and he survives by virtue in part of the wisdom and friendship of the man whose brother he has killed. Steinbeck portrays three unusually wise men in *To a God Unknown,* Joseph Wayne, Father Angelo, who is also learned, and Juanito, who, like Joseph, is quietly very brave and strong without being fierce.

Juan Chicoy in *The Wayward Bus,* the action taking place just after World War II, is significantly half Irish, half Mexican, which is to say of some Indian blood. His piety resides largely in his confidential monologues addressed to the patron saint of Mexicans, la Guadalupana, the Virgin of Guadalupe. Like Juanito, Juan is married and remains faithful, in his way, to his wife. Like Juanito, the ranch hand, Juan is regularly and gainfully employed, not as a ranch hand, but as an entrepreneur. He is a small businessman. He runs a one-bus line and a service-station garage. He owns a restaurant of sorts. He is a skilled mechanic and enjoys the performance of work, as he enjoys his management of relations with other people, on account of its elegance. Above all else, his conduct of life is characterized by style. He is generous with his assistant, with his squire apprentice, Pimples Carson. He respects the "dignidad" of Pimples and teaches him, among other things, how to drive and maintain an ancient bus, and how to treat people realistically. Pimples responds by remarking to himself: "God damn! . . . There is a man. Why'd I ever work for anybody else?"

Juan is in truth "muy hombre." Son of a Mexican revolutionary killed in Torreon, he is a sober, non-military hero who has substituted work and business enterprise for warfare. As amorist he is such a man as can, by merely looking at her, inspire Mildred Pritchard to say to herself:

> This was a man, . . . a man of complete manners. This was the kind of a man that a . . . woman would want to have because he wouldn't even want to be part woman. He would be content with his own sex. He wouldn't ever try to understand women and that would be a relief.

But if Steinbeck presents Juan as a romantic hero in the eyes of Pimples and Mildred and even in the eyes of Alice Chicoy, he presents him also, in his own eyes as a self-directing person, as a man who "could take care of himself," "not a man who fooled himself very much." Thus, having satisfactorily exchanged amorous favors with Mildred, Juan returns to Alice because she:

> . . . was the only woman he had ever found outside of Mexico who could cook beans. . . . But there was another reason too. She loved him. She really did. And he knew it. And you can't leave a thing like that. It's a structure and it has an architecture, and you can't leave it without tearing off a piece of yourself. . . . So if you want to remain whole you stay no matter how much you may dislike staying.

Juan, who does not fool himself very much, returns from errant adventure to Alice somewhat after the realistic manner of Cabell's Jurgen. I should like to suggest that there is possibly no other character in his fiction, with the exception of Doc, that Steinbeck appears to admire more openly than he does Juan Chicoy.

The last of these three pairs of characters, one Anglo, one Mexican-American, is in some ways the most intriguing since it involves comparison of Joseph and Mary Rivas, former leader of a Los Angeles Pachuco gang, with Steinbeck's Doc. Joseph and Mary Rivas is a post World War II immigrant to Cannery Row. Like Doc, and like Juan Chicoy, he is a small business-man. He has bought Lee Chong's grocery store and runs it profitably. He is a sometime labor-contractor serving, while preying upon, bracero field hands. He serves as booking agent for his nephew Cacahuete's mariachi-type musical group, Las Espaldas Mojadas.

Joseph and Mary exhibits style. Mack describes him as a "classy dresser." He is a realist; he knows that "the only person you can trust is an absolutely selfish person." He is, like Juan Chicoy, a competent judge of women. Steinbeck writes of him: "If you wanted a quick assay on a babe you couldn't ask for better than Joseph and Mary's." The Patron is also a wistful idealist: "Somewhere he felt there was a profession illegal

enough to satisfy him morally and yet safe enough not to outrage his instinctive knowledge of the law of averages, . . . a
profession [for example] wherein the victim was the partner of
the predator." He aspires in effect to achieving a commensal
refinement of the gross predator-victim relationship, one more
elegantly social, longer lasting, safer and less strenuous, one, in
the last analysis, more conservative of the integrity of both the
victim and the predator.

As amorist Joseph and Mary is an appropriate foil-compet-
itor with Doc for the attention and favor of Suzy, one opposite
and yet equal, or nearly so. For, as Steinbeck says, "Doc and
Joseph and Mary were about as opposite as you can get, but
delicately opposite. Their differences balanced like figures of a
mobile in a light breeze." And they become friends. After their
fight over Suzy, they share a pint of Old Tennis Shoes, it being
understood that Suzy is Doc's girl.

Like Doc, Joseph and Mary is unusually intelligent and
somewhat amused. He and Doc are both, in this respect, much
like Juan Chicoy, who "could see and judge and consider and
enjoy" people. Joseph and Mary's piety is as limited, in its different way, as Doc's, and as secular. Doc enjoys studying nature
and listening to what Mack calls "churchy music." Joseph and
Mary approves of "confession and forgiveness" and at least
while under the tutelage of Father Murphy did succeed "in
keeping his hands off church property."

Despite his perverse ethic, it would be a mistake to suggest
that the idealistic Joseph and Mary is not presented as an admirable, colorful, and romantic character. He is handsome, intelligent, and friendly. His business activities are scarcely more
illegal than those of any other entrepreneur, Anglo or *paisano*.
He is a logical development of the rogue hero as character moving from Danny through Juan Chicoy and illustrating in his
own person the essential abilities necessary to merge successfully with habitat which Steinbeck celebrates in all men who
are capable of doing so, abilities learned by Joseph and Mary in

ghetto Los Angeles and cultivated to admirable refinement in Monterey.

I should like to suggest by way of some attempt at conclusion that in portraying Mexican-American characters Steinbeck covered a considerable range of personality types and occupations, and demonstrated a fair variety of adjustments, mostly successful, made by his characters to their Monterey County environment.

I should like to add, as I have already intimated earlier, that in presenting his Mexican-American characters, Steinbeck has also projected toward his readers his own views of adequate human adjustment and prevalence, his own views of an adequate life style, a style grounded in the assumption that, whatever the environment, graceful conduct of life is the highest art, and that for a writer its highest performance is to portray "morally, esthetically, historically," such graceful conduct.*

---

* Footnote on Mack and the Boys: Although Steinbeck promised in his 1937 "Foreword" to *Tortilla Flat* to refrain from exposing the good people, the *paisanos*, of his fiction to harm by ever again telling any of their stories, and though literally he kept that promise for the rest of his life, he did not give up presenting in his fiction the carefree and admirable types of characters they represent. Transformed, perhaps Anglicised, they appear again in *Cannery Row* and *Sweet Thursday* as Mack and the boys, Jones, Hazel, Eddie, Whitey Number 1, Whitey Number 2, Gay, Hughie. If they had been given last names, such as Steinbeck gave to undeveloped characters such as Sparky Evea and Jimmy Brucia in *Cannery Row*, or first names like Jesus Maria Corcoran in *Tortilla Flat*, we might be able to tell whether the boys are still *paisanos* or not. I suspect that Steinbeck didn't want his readers to know, nor to care, since his principal concern with such characters was social, moral, esthetic, rather than ethnic.

ROBERT DEMOTT

STEINBECK AND THE CREATIVE PROCESS:
First Manifesto to End the Bringdown Against *Sweet Thursday*

> Don't pretend to be something you ain't, and don't make like you
> know something you don't, or sooner or later you'll fall on your
> ass.
>
> (Fauna)

I. FIRST FACTS

ARTISTS, HAWTHORNE NOTED in *The Marble Faun,* are fond of
painting their own portraits; and Wallace Stevens has written
in "The Man With the Blue Guitar" that "Poetry is the subject
of the poem." Both of these concepts, somewhat modified and
convoluted by his individual consciousness, are situated at the
heart of John Steinbeck's *Sweet Thursday.* Taken together and
in conjunction with other premises to be discussed shortly, I
submit that these ideas provide a new and profitable approach
to one of Steinbeck's most maligned and neglected novels.

Artists, specifically painters, have long been known to sit
for portraits by their own hand. In the fifteenth century artists
took delight in sneaking their own faces into their paintings of
religious and historical events. Gradually emboldened, they
stepped out in the first person with unmistakable self-portraits.
But even in these they often played parts, assuming the roles
of dandies, romantic heroes, even debauchers. Or they appeared in symbolic guise: Titian served up his own head on Sa-
lome's platter; Michaelangelo left his own face on St. Barthole-
mew's flayed skin. At times they used themselves as painting
props for experiments in new techniques and styles like Par-
migianino, a Renaissance painter of Parma who produced a
self-portrait on a convex panel which so impressed Pope Clem-
ent VII he was readily offered a job in Rome. The urge to paint
the painter, as it were, has continued unbroken to present time

157

from its early beginnings through such notable performances as William Hogarth's self homage done in 1745 in which he depicts himself in a picture within a picture, to artists like Pierre Bonnard and Joan Miró who both produced fascinating portraits of themselves in 1938: the former conceptualizing his frail frame in violent splotches of color, the latter utilizing surrealist lines and symbols to depict himself in flux.

The presence of the artist in fiction and poetry, however, does not have the lengthy tradition painting can claim. One need not go back much further than the late eighteenth century to discover generations of writers entirely uninterested in their own careers as subject matter. Since then, and especially in our own times, we have become familiar with the artist-hero whose difficult relationship to life is the master problem of the author. "In the last century and a half we have become accustomed to find the poet overtly present in his poems," George Wright notes;[1] or the novelist in his novel, one might add. The modern theme of the artist's alienation—as we see it in Mann, Gide, and Joyce, for instance—is an outgrowth of the nineteenth century myth of the artist as a special species. He may be angel or demon, but he never wants to be considered merely man. Ultimately, however, this is not quite right, for as Maurice Beebe comments, "Although the artist-hero claims individuality in that he is different from the majority of men, his quest for true self usually ends in the discovery that he is very much like other artists, that in fact he embodies the archetype of the artist."[2]

It might be argued, then, that an artist's view of artists is of intimate importance for the rest of mankind. If he succeeds in explaining the nature and causes of his own activities—their aim

---

[1] *The Poet in the Poem: The Personae of Eliot, Yeats, and Pound* (Berkeley: University of California Press, 1960; paper edition, University of California Press, 1962), p. 93.

[2] *Ivory Towers and Sacred Founts* (New York: New York University Press, 1964), p. 6.

and their product, their gratification and their cost—he is capable of telling us more than another might about the conception men generally hold of themselves in his time, and of the relation in his society between the individual and the social, the unique and the characteristic, the intellectual and the practical powers. A portrait of the artist, to quote Beebe again,

> . . . helps us to understand the novelist who wrote it. The novel can be seen in much the same manner as the writer's letters, diaries, notebooks, prefaces, or memoirs—though, of course, the careful critic will not make a one-to-one equation between a work of art and an autobiography. Nonetheless, the very fact that the artist-novel is a product of the imagination, in which the experience it uses is distorted and transcended, makes it often more revealing than primary documents, for writers frequently tell more about their true selves and convictions under the guise of fiction than they will confess publicly.[3]

Perhaps an artist's "portrait of the artist" will be, as the phrase suggests, a self-portrait, with lineaments of joy and anguish very like his own. But it is also apt to be a portrait not only of himself as artist but as man—possibly idealized and rationalized—but nevertheless significant for its attention to his major preoccupation—the persona portrayed as an intellectual or craftsman, as idealist or careerist, even (in Steinbeck's case) as scientist. Thus the artist passes judgment, so to speak, through this portrait, upon that matrix of human impulses and situations which twine themselves about his unique creative thrust. He shows us the way to live by telling us how he lives.

II. PARALLELS MUST BE RELATED

Fine, you say. But what has all of this got to do with Steinbeck? Well, just this. Endless numbers of artist-hero novels exist in American and British literature and we all know, as William York Tindall claims, that "from 1903 onwards, almost

---

[3] *Ibid.*, pp. 4-5.

every first novel by a serious novelist was a novel of adoles-
cence,"[4] that is, it focused on a sensitive young man who is a
potential artist or novelist. But what of those works where the
thematic focus is on other preoccupations than the chronological
coming to maturity of the youthful protagonist, and the artist-
figure, perhaps already aged or grown, is hidden or ostensibly
obscured by a deceptive welter of practical problems the central character finds it necessary to deal with, or, as in Steinbeck's case, the artist figure is presented to us in the guise of a
scientist?

If an artist writes in what approximates a naturalistic tradition, say, as Frank Norris does in both *The Octopus* and *The
Pit,* then the figure of the artist, Presley in the former, Sheldon
Corthell in the latter, will not only be subsumed in the over-
whelming force and web of external circumstances, in the face
of which the function of art is greatly minimized or even totally
negated, but the artist figure will be scorned and ridiculed, so
to speak, as a man incapable of dealing with the sordidness and
brutalities of "real" life. If he indulges in a life of art, as Sheldon
Corthell does, his sensibilities are held to be specious or feminine at best, and it is women, not men, who are most attracted
to the artist, as Mrs. Derrick is to the poet Presley.

Steinbeck has placed himself to some degree in the naturalistic tradition, not, to be sure, always with a vengeance, but
enough so that his biological and scientific vision of life informs
his work and helps delineate his characters. But somehow to
say this is inadequate, for despite Steinbeck's biological focus,
which naturally connotes the objectivity and dispassion of a
scientist, he has always insisted on viewing the whole of reality.
He wrote in *The Log From the Sea of Cortez* the need "to go
wide open. Let's see what we see, record what we find, and not
fool ourselves with conventional scientific strictures . . . . Let
us . . . not be betrayed by this myth of permanent objective

---

[4] *Forces in Modern British Literature, 1885-1946* (New York: Alfred
Knopf, 1947), p. 176.

reality."[5] Lester Marks understands Steinbeck's biologist hero knows objective reality "is only part of the truth," and therefore must allow himself "the luxury of subjectivity."[6] If Steinbeck has gone this far in his conception of the scientist, that is, in his radically humanizing the scientist as man, then is it wrong to say his next step, perhaps the logical one, is to a portrait of the artist, or at least to a presentation of the condition of the artist masked by the realist's respect for and awe of the scientist?

As the evidence in *Journal of a Novel* reveals, Steinbeck was frontally engaged with the enigmas of artistic creation in the early 1950's and I believe he was too shrewd to make any final distinction between authentic artist and scientist.[7] The struggle to create and invent are similar in both types, and since he was more at home, so to speak, with the personality and method of the scientist, having already established Doc as a viable fictional character in his works, he integrated and projected his own struggle with the demon of creativity into Doc who metamorphosed into scientist-as-artist and vice versa. In his new guise Doc can, as Peter Lisca writes, become "a closer expression" of Steinbeck's present attitudes, attitudes which might have been disapproved of by Doc's prototype, Ed Ricketts.[8] "The design of a book," Steinbeck announced in the opening paragraph of *The Log from the Sea of Cortez*, "is the pattern

---

[5] (New York: Viking Press, 1951), p. 1. Subsequent references will be included in the text of my paper.

[6] *Thematic Design in the Novels of John Steinbeck* (The Hague: Mouton, 1969), p. 18.

[7] Cf. Emerson's comment, written in 1851, that there is no real difference between the scientist's and the artist's inspiration. "There is and must be a little air-chamber, a sort of tiny Bedlam in even the naturalist's or mathematician's brain who arrives at great results. They affect a sticking to facts; they repudiate all imagination and affection as they would stealing. But . . . [they] . . . must all have this spark of fanaticism for generation of steam. . . ." *Journals of Ralph Waldo Emerson*, eds. E. W. Emerson and W. E. Forbes (Boston: Houghton Mifflin, 1909-1914), VIII, 177.

[8] *The Wide World of John Steinbeck* (Brunswick, New Jersey: Rutgers University Press, 1958), p. 282.

of a reality controlled and shaped by the mind of the writer. This is completely understood about poetry or fiction, but it is too seldom realized about books of fact. And yet the impulse which drives a man to poetry will send another man into the tide pools and force him to try to report what he finds there" (1). The identification between scientist and artist is thus complete in Steinbeck's mind. The means, method, and rationale are co-equal for both types; only the ends differ.

In *Sweet Thursday* Steinbeck pays public homage to artistry. Even though he has no strict artist-heroes in his fiction, that is, no central protagonists who are solely artists and earn their living writing or painting, and while certain artistic types like the novelist Joe Elegant and the painter Henri are ineffectual as artists and humans, Steinbeck is able, perhaps forced, to talk at last about the problems of creativity and artistry which beset him. In *Sweet Thursday*, he manages to circumvent personal feelings of guilt or compromise over his theme by using Doc as his artistic surrogate.

Doc has long been considered Steinbeck's embodiment of the ideal scientist, but never has his centrality as an artist figure been noted. In *Sweet Thursday* Doc potentially combines the two poles of the artist necessary for creation—subjectivity and objectivity, feeling and thought—and as long as both "poles" are not coincident, Doc cannot write his paper on "Symptoms in Some Cephalopods Approximating Apoplexy." However, once subjectivity and objectivity come into proper orbit, once the divergent tendencies of the divided self of the creator become coincident, when in short, Doc becomes whole as a result of his successful courting of Suzy, his muse, and allows himself the luxury of subjectiveness, then creative productivity is imminent.

Sweet Thursday, then, is a novel about the writing of a novel, if you will allow me that indulgence. Its subject may be as banal as boy meets girl, or as contrived as the efforts of Mack and Fauna to *make sure* boy meets girl, but its theme and its deep structural principle are creativity and the condition of the artist.[9] All the banter, hilarity, and carefree nihilism centered in and around Mack and the boys cannot disguise that fact, nor, since publication of *Journal of a Novel*, can we dismiss the importance of creativity and its workings, "the straining and puffing"[10] Steinbeck called it, which occurred in his life and work in the early 1950's.

III. WHAT HAPPENED IN BETWEEN

However, more of this later. Let me now begin at the beginning. Mack's function as a literary critic in *Sweet Thursday* should be noted at the outset. What Mack says in the "Prologue" of the novel is vital because it is reflexive. "Poetry is the subject of the poem" I quoted Stevens as saying earlier, and Steinbeck perhaps very much to our surprise describes (through Mack) the very book he has just written, or is going to write, depending on when the Prologue was actually composed. While Steinbeck's particular employment of a self-reflexive and self-descriptive portrait of a novel may startle us because it seems inconsistent with our conception of the man and what he has written up to that point, there is a precedent for such actions in writers like Melville and Hawthorne. One need only recall

---

[9] I think Steinbeck's earlier short story "The Chrysanthemums" can also be read as a parable of the artist's condition in society. Elisa Allen possesses "Planter's hands," that is, a kind of creative intuition and both she and her products, the beautiful flowers, can exist only in a closed valley, a symbol of the artist's Ivory Tower. When Elisa meets the "real" world head on, represented by the tinker, she is defeated. The harsh realities of life in the 30's, Steinbeck implies, have no patience with artistic and feminine ephemera. Henry Allen puts up with his wife's idiosyncrasies, but wishes she would turn her creative powers to growing larger and better apples for the Allens to sell profitably. If my "reading" of this story is valid, the transition Steinbeck made in utilizing the theme of creativity and the condition of the artist-scientist in *Sweet Thursday* is more vividly underscored, because it is not treated harshly or scornfully.

[10] (New York: Viking Press, 1969), p. 4. Subsequent references will be included in the text of my discussion.

Ishmael's confrontation with the strange painting hanging over the bar at the Spouter Inn in Chapter 3 of *Moby Dick:* that puzzling and confounding "long limber, portentous, black mass of something" so compelling Ishmael says that "you involuntarily took an oath with yourself to find out what that marvellous painting meant." Of the five possible explanations Ishmael offers for the painting, none of them seem complete until the viewer can ascertain the meaning of "one portentous something in the picture's midst. *That* once found out," he continues, "and all the rest were plain." But even discovering the *that* may be the great leviathan himself is no guarantee of understanding the meaning of the canvas. So it is, Melville is saying, with our understanding of the book he is writing. Hawthorne, too, engages in similar literary strategies. Think back on "The Custom House Sketch" of the *Scarlet Letter* when the narrator discovers Hester's (herself a surrogate artist) scarlet A, wrought with such wonderful skill that his eyes "fastened themselves upon the old scarlet letter, and would not be turned aside." Just as generations of readers have been fascinated by Hawthorne's novel, so for the narrator there was some deep meaning in the letter, "most worthy of interpretation, and which, as it were, steamed forth from the mystic symbol, subtly communicating itself" to his sensibilities, but evading the analysis of . . . [his] . . . mind." Both Melville and Hawthorne iconographically presented the heart of the meaning of the novel they are engaged in writing in order to make us realize the importance and centrality the creative act assumed in their lives. Maybe including Steinbeck in such august company as Melville, Hawthorne, and Stevens seems unduly harsh on them, yet I am certain Steinbeck's presentation of a literary apologia in the comic, even satiric, guise of Mack is his first indication in *Sweet Thursday* that literary creativity is the theme and substance of this novel.

Mack's aesthetic is based on three points: (1) chapter headings, (2) selective description and dialogue, and (3) hooptedoodle, or unrelated materials. "I guess I'm just a critic,"

Mack begins. "But if I ever come across the guy that wrote that book [*Cannery Row*] I could tell him a few things." Mack was not satisfied with *Cannery Row;* he would have written it differently. What Mack symbolizes is Steinbeck's desire to draw attention to his rationale and methodology in *Sweet Thursday* and the changes wrought there that differentiate it from *Cannery Row*. The first requisite Mack insists on is that each chapter have a title:

> Suppose there's chapter one, chapter two, chapter three. That's all right, as far as it goes, but I'd like to have a couple of words at the top so it tells me what the chapter's going to be about. Sometimes maybe I want to go back, and chapter five don't mean nothing to me. If there was just a couple of words I'd know that was the chapter I wanted to go back to.[11]

What Mack demands, Steinbeck provides. Not only is it easier for the general reader to go back and know by the chapter heading which chapter he wants to reread, but Good Lord! it may be the first time Steinbeck has done anything to help the literary critic who also finds individual titles make the chapters more accessible.

Next, Mack wants "a lot of talk in a book" but he doesn't want to "have nobody tell me what the guy that's talking looks like. I want to figure out what he looks like from the way he talks." Admittedly this is a bit difficult in *Sweet Thursday* because Mack knows everyone already. But as a fictional stratagem for Steinbeck's readers and as a general literary principle, it is quite viable. In chapter five, for instance, Joe Blaikey, Monterey's constable, is barely described by Steinbeck, yet by his immediate sizing up of Suzy and his direct, pointed interrogation of her, and finally his offer that "If you need a buck to blow town, come to me" (24), one can ascertain, I think, what kind of character Joe is—certainly he is kind and concerned and his

---

[11] John Steinbeck, *Sweet Thursday* (New York: Viking Press, 1954; paper edition, New York: Bantam Books, 1963). The Prologue is not paginated. Wherever applicable, all page references to the novel will appear in my essay.

directness bespeaks a man who is hard, determined and tough, maybe lean and spare. Obviously, this is speculation on my part. I can imagine you muttering to yourselves, "DeMott, DeMott, you have much to answer for!" But before you throw up your hands in utter despair, think of this: If Joe conjures up another appearance to each one of you, then Steinbeck's method (and Mack's requisite) that the reader participate in the novel by re-creating the character from the brief materials offered, is a success. What Mack wants and what Steinbeck strives to provide is a literature of process wherein the impact of human involvement is co-equal in both book and reader.[12] As witnesses we are forced to participate in the fabric of the book's meaning by helping create that meaning for ourselves. William Carlos Williams said it best in *Spring and All:* "In the imagination we are from henceforth (so long as you read) locked in fraternal embrace, the classic caress of author and reader. We are one. Whenever I say 'I' I mean also 'you.' And so, together, as one, we shall begin."

Mack has other requirements for fiction. He wants to figure out what a "guy's thinking by what he says," and he wants "some description too. He wants to know what color a thing is, how it smells and maybe how it looks, and maybe how a guy feels about it—but not too much of that." Steinbeck provides all of this, again in chapter five, where he describes Suzy and her subsequent conversation with Joe Blaikey. Steinbeck

---

[12] Charles Feidelson has addressed himself to this idea in considering poetry, but his comment is such that it fits neatly Steinbeck's method too: "A poem, therefore, instead of referring to a completed act of perception, constitutes the act itself, both in the author and in the reader; instead of describing reality, a poem is a realization." *Symbolism and American Literature* (Chicago: University of Chicago Press, 1953; paper edition, University of Chicago Press, 1962), p. 18. Elisa Allen's discovery of the tinker's treachery in throwing away her chrysanthemum shoots and keeping the pot they were contained in has ironic impact co-equal for Elisa and the reader. We become aware of the act and its implications just at the moment she does.

sketches Suzy factually in one cogent paragraph providing the kind of description Mack wants, based greatly on the color of things:

> Suzy was a pretty girl with a flat nose and a wide mouth. She had a good figure, was twenty-one, five-feet-five, hair probably brown (dyed blond), brown cloth coat, rabbit skin collar, cotton print dress, brown calf shoes (heel taps a little run over), scuff on the right toe. She limped slightly on her right foot (23).

Even Mack would be pleased at this rendering because despite Steinbeck's illusion of completeness in initially portraying Suzy, and our eventual realization she is a whore, this is still only a partial picture of the woman and hardly accounts for the gutsiness and fortitude she evidences later in the novel. In short, she is capable of surprising us.[13] In the ensuing dialogue with Joe, Suzy is evasive and noncommittal, allowing us (or inviting us) to figure out what the character is thinking by what she says:

> Joe said quietly to Suzy, "What's on your mind, sister?"
> "Not a thing," said Suzy. She didn't look at him but she could see him in the shine of a malted machine behind the counter.
> "Vacation?"
> "Sure."
> "How long?"
> "Don't know."
> "Looking for a job?"
> "Maybe" (23).

What Suzy is thinking and what she learns are not immediately articulated. They are withheld while the effects of her meeting with Joe work upon us. Later, in chapter 22, Fauna gives pragmatic advice to Suzy which echoes Mack's literary concern: "If a guy says something that picks up your interest," Fauna instructs, "why, don't hide it from him. Kind of try to

---

[13] Cf. Steinbeck's comment in *Journal of a Novel:* "If a man has a too pat style, his reader can after a little time keep ahead of him. I mean the reader will know what is coming by how it is done. And I am trying to remove this possibility by constant change" (62).

wonder what he's thinking instead of how you're going to answer him back" (94). Steinbeck does some of the work necessary to create the proper atmosphere and to portray character, but not so much that he cheats the reader out of experiencing and participating in the imaginative recreation of the novel and its characters.

There is a final point in Mack's aesthetic. He tells Whiteys No. 1 and 2 and Eddie that:

> Sometimes I want a book to break loose with a bunch of hooptedoodle. The guy's writing it give him a chance to do a little hooptedoodle. Spin up some pretty words maybe, or sing a little song with language. That's nice. But I wish it was set aside so I don't have to read it. I don't want hooptedoodle to get mixed up in the story. So if the guy that's writing it wants hooptedoodle, he ought to put it right at first. Then I can skip it if I want to, or maybe go back to it after I know how the story come out.

At this point we might be inclined to forget that Steinbeck wrote *Sweet Thursday*, not Mack. Lest we should forget, Steinbeck deliberately has not followed Mack's "advice" to the letter. True, Steinbeck includes a chapter entitled "Hooptedoodle (I)" in the first 20 pages of the novel; however, it does not contain unrelated materials, but instead focuses on the change in Doc since the *Cannery Row* days. The chapter emphasizes Doc's need for "reorientation" (20) in a changing world and tells us of his intention to write a scientific paper. Later Steinbeck writes two authentic hooptedoodle chapters: "The Great Roque War" (chapter 8) and "Hooptedoodle (2), or the Pacific Grove Butterfly Festival" (chapter 38), including in them materials which have no organic relation to the novel; chapters which one can skip if one wants to, or maybe go back to after he knows "how the story come out."

What is the point of Steinbeck's convoluting Mack's literary advice in this way? I do not think it is evidence of Steinbeck's inability to carry out his own proposal as outlined in the Prologue. Rather, it is further evidence that *Sweet Thursday* can be read as a fable of the artist. Steinbeck is telling us that no matter what *we* think about the relation of the artist to his work, *he* is ineluctably central to his novel. He can throw us off the track by "violating" Mack's credo to prove beyond a doubt he is in control of his materials. This is *Sweet Thursday* he is exclaiming: sole owner and proprietor, John Steinbeck. The novelist, Steinbeck implies, stands at the center of the world he creates. He is central to and definitive of the reality he perceives, and in perceiving re-creates. As such, the author can call his own shots. He can end his novel with a chapter on mayonnaise, simply because he has always wanted to end a novel with a chapter on mayonnaise, as Richard Brautigan had done in *Trout Fishing in America;* or he can violate his own reflexive credo as Steinbeck does to show that as artist he is master of all he surveys and creates. "A foolish consistency" Emerson noted in "Self-Reliance," "is the hobgoblin of little minds;" and Whitman, too, provides a gloss on our text from "Song of Myself:" "Do I contradict myself? Very well . . . I am large, I contain multitudes."

In *Journal of a Novel* Steinbeck makes an assertion about his presence in *East of Eden,* and it is of such validity it is equally applicable to *Sweet Thursday:*

> . . . a book—at least the kind of book I am writing—should contain everything that seems to me to be true. There are few enough true things in the world. It would be a kind of sin to conceal any of them or to hide their little heads in technique as the squeamishness of not appearing in one's own book. For many years I did not occur in my writing. But this was only apparently true—I was in them every minute. I just didn't seem to be. But in this book I am in it and I don't for a moment pretend not to be (24).[14]

To paraphrase a sub-sub librarian of my acquaintance, this all sounds haughtily egocentric if it were not for the fact that it is so curiously centric. Steinbeck is right to speak of his presence in *East of Eden* as the "I" who depends "on hearsay, on old

---

[14] Cf. Steinbeck's comment in the imaginary dialogue between the writer and his editors in the original draft for the Dedication of *East of Eden* in *Journal of a Novel:* "Goddamn it. This is my book. I'll make the children talk any way I want" (181).

photographs, on stories told, and on memories which are hazy and mixed with fable"[15] in weaving the story of the Hamiltons. His centrality in that novel is explicit. He exists as himself in *East of Eden*, recreating his own history as he goes. In *Sweet Thursday* the impulse is the same, but the vehicle is different. The "I" of the central consciousness never blatantly intrudes because he is subsumed in the persona characterized by Doc. Nevertheless, because Doc's preoccupations, especially the struggle inherent in creativity, are so personally Steinbeck's, it is tempting to say he is the proper artistic surrogate, the "I" perceived omnisciently, if you will, around which the book and its theme fruitfully revolve.

IV. THE CREATIVE CROSS

The artist's process of creation is cyclical. In order to create a work the artist must suffer a half-phase of psychic dislocation in which he is stripped of his old ways of viewing the world. He must reduce himself to a condition of figurative ignorance which will allow him to see and react to the things of his world clearly and simply. This, however, is not enough, for it is only one-half of the cycle. The greatest significance of the creative act is contained in the self-surpassing goal—the proper combination of words, ideas, and images which constitute the created work. The artistic product comes as a result of the artist's return from his descent, or the symbolic extrication from his immediate engagement with reality. The artist, George Whalley writes, "must 'return' from his vision . . . his immersion in reality as a *condition of survival* . . . . The only way he can return is to transfer his experience of immersion to a physical artefact: and that is his half-phase of 'action,' his return to the social world."[16] By focusing on Doc, Steinbeck presents us with the cyclical

---

[15] (New York: Viking Press, 1952; paper edition, New York: Bantam Books, 1955), p. 5.

[16] *The Poetic Process: An Essay in Poetics* (New York: World Publishing Company, 1967), p. 117.

process of creativity which is somewhat transmogrified because it is incomplete. Doc suffers the first phase of the cycle, the descent to the bottom, but only part of the second stage for reasons we shall soon see.

There can be no creation without destruction. There is and can be no such thing as authentic artistic creation until the *bon trucs* of reality are annihilated as thoroughly as possible by the vast and painful process of un-thinking which ultimately may result in a new relationship between the artist and his world. The first step the artist is obliged to make is the formation of a new and original relationship with the universe, which can become the occasion for consciousness and self-discovery. As Brewster Ghiselin has perceptively established:

> The whole activity of the mind always transcends the specific activity that forms the pattern of any moment of consciousness. The mind, moreover, belongs to time—at least when it is sane. The maintenance of its sanity requires its orderly implication in the processes of the world. And therefore it must give itself to change. The order inherited from any preceding moment often will not perfectly adjust it to the realities of the present moment, the pressures of the instant. Then, to make possible a new adjustment, the closed system of the inherited order—the accepted pattern of consciousness—must be broken. Of itself it will not alter, it must be penetrated from without. It must be washed over, flooded, drowned, and perhaps dissolved, in the greater activity of the whole mind. This is the disordering that makes order possible, out of which all living order comes.[17]

Doc, I suggest, goes through a similar re-ordering experience. After his discharge from the Army, he returns to the Row to find everything changed and his laboratory—a symbol of his pre-war life—in shambles. "Change was everywhere. People were gone, or changed, and that was almost like being gone," Steinbeck writes (2). Before the war Doc carried on a collecting business. He was a benign person with "few responsibilities except to be a kindly, generous, and amused man" (13). But after

---

[17] "The Birth of a Poem," in *The Creative Process*, ed. Brewster Ghiselin (Berkeley: University of California Press, 1952; paper edition, New York: New American Library, n.d.), p. 128.

returning to the Row Doc is discontent and restless. He suddenly realizes the need to satisfy himself by finding out who he is and what he is capable of. Even at this early point he is beginning to suffer the loneliness and isolation of the artist. "Quest for self," Maurice Beebe says, "is the dominant theme of the artist-novel, and because the self is always in conflict with society, a closely related theme is the opposition of art to life. The artist-as-hero is usually therefore the artist-as-exile."[18] In Doc's case he consciously chooses a direction he feels will redeem himself from loneliness and rebuild his floundering self-concept: he elects the creator's salvation of writing a paper over the social salvation of marrying. "Like I was saying, Doc. Everybody in the Row is worried about you. You don't have no fun. You wander around like you was lost," Mack says, then adds, "you need a dame" (20). But Doc quickly responds: "I'm all right, Mack. Don't let anybody give me a wife though—don't let them give me a wife! I guess a man needs direction. That's what I've been needing" (20). Doc's source of direction, however, is not Mack's. He says proudly, "I'm going to call my paper 'Symptoms in Some Cephalopods Approximating Apoplexy.'" Before this lofty resolution Mack is nearly speechless. "Great God Almighty," he says in awe.

Chapter six of *Sweet Thursday* presents in real and metaphoric terms a synecdoche of the artist figure at work and introduces the real theme of Steinbeck's novel. Simply stated, creativity is difficult work. The writer needs iron self-discipline to resist the seductions of procrastinating—the endless frying of eggs for dinner, staring at the yellow pad under the hanging light, the sharpening and resharpening of pencils, the urge to get up and look out the study window. "I'll work my head off to avoid work," Doc admits to himself (29). Finally, though, he picks up his pencil and writes a short paragraph, but then terminates it abruptly when his pencil breaks. "He took another, and it broke with a jerk." Even his first start is a false one, while

---

[18] *Ivory Towers and Sacred Founts*, p. 6.

slowly the realization that can cripple the artist flashes in his mind: perhaps he has "nothing to say" (29).[19]

Frightened by this knowledge, Doc begins to brood about his inability to "take everything I've seen and thought and learned and reduce them and relate them until I have something of meaning, something of use" (47). His failure is that he "can't seem to do it" (47). In order to create, the artist-surrogate must possess a sound knowledge of his own self-concept, but paradoxically, his selfhood is affirmed through the act of creation. As Jaques Maritain asserts:

> The essential need of the poet is to create; but he cannot do so without passing through the door of the knowing, as obscure as it may be, of his own subjectivity. For poetry means first of all an intellective act which by its essence is creative, and forms something into being . . . and what can such an intellective act possibly express and manifest in producing the work if not the very being and substance of the one who creates?[20]

Doc resists the will power needed to perform his task and instead gives in to the ease of collecting starfish—a mechanical operation for him—which makes him "glad to do the old and practical work" (55). Later, making a starfish embryo series, another mechanical task, he notes the "safety in the known thing—no speculation here" (63); little chance for error, but then, little chance for creative success. His seduction has been complete, at least for a time. "His old life came back to him—a plateau of contentment with small peaks of excitement but none of the pain of original thinking, none of the loneliness of invention" (64).

---

[19] Cf. Steinbeck's comment in *Journal of a Novel*. "It must be told that my second work day is a bust as far as getting into the writing. I suffer as always from the fear of putting down the first line. It is amazing the terrors, the magics, the prayers, the straightening shyness that assails one" (9).

[20] *Creative Intuition in Art and Poetry* (New York: World Publishing Company, 1966), p. 82. While Maritain specifically speaks of the making of poetry in his quotation, I take the liberty to apply its fundamental meaning to the creative act encompassing both scientist and artist as Steinbeck does.

Doc's mental flabbiness, his seductive comfort, are inimical to authentic creativity. In order for him to descend much, much further into himself and his materials, he must make a great, courageous leap and abnegate the old order of existence. As creator he must suffer to earn his beatitude; his brains or his guts or wherever he writes from must bleed forth the new reality of creation which from that moment on becomes the only reality. His life can no longer be defined in terms of what he has done or been, but in terms of what he must do.[21] At some point he must have his "last bounce on the board, the last look into the pool" (*Journal of a Novel*, p. 12) before the dive. For Doc the first shock of consciousness comes from Suzy. She tells him in the seventeenth chapter that everyone is laughing at him behind his back because he cannot write his paper. After Doc faces the truth given him by a whore, he can once again make a start on his essay. But outside intervention—this time Old Jingleballicks—causes another interruption and Doc is put off. Old Jay, however, proves a wise fool. His purpose seems to be to get Doc thinking about both his paper and his personal condition. Doc's admission of fear at beginning the paper prompts Jay to tell him "There's a lack of fulfillment in you" (123), by which he means Doc needs a woman, perhaps Suzy. Of course, Doc reacts vehemently to this and denies anything other than a scientific interest in Suzy. Jay, however, is not convinced and neither, I might add, is the reader.

V. IN WHICH NOTHING IS CONCLUDED

The situation continues apace on the Row. The wild party and mortgage scheme of Mack and the boys provides a farcical counterpoint to a disintegrating and drifting Doc who is still

---

[21] In *Journal of a Novel* Steinbeck continually noted he wanted to write *East of Eden* as though it were his last book, that is, as though everything depended on it. "This is the one to come," he said. "There is nothing beyond this book—nothing follows it. It must contain all in the world I know and it must have everything in it which I am capable . . ." (8).

unable to face himself squarely. Doc and Suzy, nearly "married" in a slapstick masquerade ceremony, move apart and provide further contrast in their life styles. While Doc undergoes "Reorganization so profound he didn't know it was happening" (132), that is, unconscious change, Suzy is proving her worth by walking away from the horror of the mock marriage determined to rebuild herself and her world from the inside out, organically, to be ready for Doc.[22]

Meanwhile, the thirtieth chapter comes and goes and Doc is still unable to write his essay. He has, however, learned one thing. He lacks love, both the giving of it and the receiving of it. He knows Suzy can be the source of these emotions, but still his stubborn streak, symbolized by the analytical and objective self, will not admit Suzy's worth:

> Not only is she illiterate, but she has a violent temper. She has all of the convictions of the uninformed. She is sure of things she has not investigated, not only sure for herself, but sure for everyone. In two months she will become a prude. Then where will freedom go? (155)

Life is best felt upon the pulse Keats wrote; Doc's subjective self, the private artistic man who represents his true feelings, hoots in agreement: "You can't *not* have it too. Whatever happens, you've got her. Take a feel of your pulse, listen to your pounding heart" (155). Doc does listen when the floodgates of human emotion open to wash away his old prejudices and narrow conception of life. In an epiphanic moment Doc sees clearly

---

[22] Steinbeck's emphasis on reclamation of people and things is an essential part of his fable of creativity. He is instructing us in the ways of finding the proper materials needed for art. Suzy's boiler, for instance, represents the raw and unattractive rock of reality; yet when imagination casts its veil over the cold iron, it is transformed into a viable and necessary product: literally, a home for Suzy; metaphorically, an architectural symbol which implies both the means and ends of artistic construction and the imagination. The transformation of the Palace Flophouse and its inhabitants on the night of the masquerade and the emphasis that Suzy is more than an ordinary prostitute are chapters in the same lesson.

what he must do. He responds by performing an uncharacteristic and jealous (but entirely human) act. At 3:17 in the morning, Doc rushes out and beats up Joseph and Mary Rivas who has been hanging lecherously around Suzy's boiler-home. Finally, then, Doc has committed himself to action and to a new life.

Doc knows there can be no turning back now: "I am not whole without her. When she was with me I was more alive than I have ever been, and not only when she was pleasant either. Even when we were fighting I was whole. . . . Over and over, I'll wish I'd never seen her. But I also know that if I fail I'll never be a whole man. I'll live a gray half-life, and I'll mourn for my lost girl every hour of the rest of my life" (161).[23] Shortly after emerging from his lab, having fought an internal battle with cowardice, he heads to Suzy's boiler. The lesson he learns from Suzy there is even greater than he learned from Bach.[24]

> Old Bach had his talent and his family and his friends. Everyone has something. And what has Suzy got? Absolutely nothing in the world but guts. She's taken on an atomic world with a slingshot, and, by God, she's going to win. If she doesn't win there's no point in living any more" (162).

---

[23] Concerning the love of a woman in the artist novel, Maurice Beebe writes in *Ivory Towers and Sacred Founts,* "In many artist-novels—James' *Roderick Hudson,* Flaubert's *Sentimental Education,* and Gissing's *New Grub Street* . . . the artist is destroyed as artist because of his submission to love. In other novels, the artist feels that he cannot function without love. Hardy's *The Well-Beloved,* Wyndham Lewis's *Tarr,* Dreiser's *The Genius'* . . . are examples of the novels in which the artist-hero must have romantic fulfillment to produce. . . ." (18). *Sweet Thursday* may be profitably added to Beebe's list.

[24] Suzy functions as a personal equivalent of the mythic source or wellspring to which the hero must return in order to gain strength. Cf. Mircea Eliade's comment in *Cosmos and History: The Myth of Eternal Return,* trans. Willard Trask (New York: Harper and Row, 1959): The road to the center, or source, is "arduous, fraught with perils, because it is, in fact, a rite of passage from the profane to the sacred, from the ephemeral and illusory to reality and eternity, from death to life. . . ." (18).

With his awareness of his need for Suzy comes a new resolution to write his paper, first by collecting needed specimens
during the spring tides at La Jolla. Doc knows he is a "dead
duck," a finished man, without his essay. All major obstacles for
its completion have been removed so he can no longer excuse or
rationalize his failure and indolence.

Doc reached the metaphoric ground-zero at the bottom of
his creative cycle. But thankfully, his vision and realization of
mutual love encountered there are beneficial and he is ready to
begin the long ascent the second phase of creativity's cycle en-
tails.[25] With Suzy by his side, it will be easier than the descent.
Whatever new obstacles Doc may encounter, Hazel's breaking
of Doc's arm, for example, Doc can overcome. Setbacks can
only be temporary at worst because he has a wholeness born of
pain, suffering, and fate that allows him to proceed in the proper
direction. Curiously though, no final product is evident. Steinbeck has withheld that, although he has shown his faith in Doc's
future by endowing him as an institution and by arranging a
reading of his paper before the California Academy of Sciences,
both ostensibly due to Old Jay.

The novel ends appropriately in spring, the time of fulfillment and growth. The tentative ending of the novel, that is, the
implied ending that Doc and Suzy will be successful, are tied to

---

[25] Carl Jung has written perceptively about the re-creation of the
self in situations similar to Doc's, where there is a return to the source that
can either debilitate the libido permanently or encourage it and nourish it.
He notes: " . . . when there is any great work to be done, from which
human being shrinks, doubting his own strength, his libido streams back to
that source—and that is a dangerous moment, the moment of decision
between destruction and a new life. If the libido remains caught in the
wonderland of the inner world, the human being becomes a mere shadow
in the upper world; he is no better than a dead man or a seriously ill one.
But if the libido succeeds in tearing itself free and struggling up to the
upper world again, then a miracle occurs, for this descent to the under-
world has been a rejuvenation for the libido and from its apparent death
a new fruitfulness has awakened." *Psychological Reflection,* ed. Jolande
Jacobi (New York: Harper and Row, 1961), p. 293.

Steinbeck's comment in *Journal of a Novel:* "I guess I am terrified to write finish on the book for fear I myself will be finished" (164).[26] Such is the case with Doc's situation. He has earned his beatitude through loneliness, shock, and his sensitivity to the lesson Suzy taught him of needed reclamation of the body and spirit when one seems most defeated. When Doc fully admits the subjective and objective poles of humanity are necessary to live and to create, he learns the most valuable lesson of his life. There was no reason for Steinbeck to carry the parable on any longer. The telling of it can end here while the effects of it go on indefinitely.

---

[26] Steinbeck's chief reason for enjoying the writing of *East of Eden* was its sense of continuation. "It is because there is no end. It goes on and on into a kind of infinity" (p. 24). M. H. Abrams' comment about organicism is pertinent here: " . . . organic growth is an open-ended process, nurturing a sense of the promise of the incomplete, and the glory of the imperfect." See *The Mirror and the Lamp: Romantic Theory and the Critical Tradition* (New York: Oxford University Press, 1953; paper edition, New York: W. W. Norton Company, 1958), p. 220.

CONTRIBUTORS

BENTON, ROBERT M. Assistant Professor of English, Central Washington State College; published in *Early American Literature, American Literature, New York Public Library Bulletin.*

DEGNAN, JAMES P. Associate Professor of English, University of Santa Clara; Beinecke Foundation award winner for public affairs writing; Pulitzer Prize nominee; published in *Atlantic Monthly, Kenyon Review, Esquire, Virginia Quarterly Review, The Nation, The Progressive, Commonweal.*

DEMOTT, ROBERT. Assistant Professor of English, Ohio University; Associate Editor, *Steinbeck Quarterly;* former National Assistant Director of *Abstracts of English Studies;* published in *Kent Quarterly, Melange, Steinbeck Quarterly.*

DITSKY, JOHN. Assistant Professor of English, University of Windsor; published in *Windsor Review, Steinbeck Quarterly, Descant, Black Moss, Southern Humanities Review, Mainline, Other Voices.*

HEDGPETH, JOEL W. Professor of Oceanography and Chief, Yaquina Marine Laboratory of the Marine Science Center at Newport of Oregon State University at Corvallis. Author of over one hundred books, articles, and essays on such topics as the Systematics and Biogeography of Pycnogonida, the Antarctic, and Welsh literature; inheritor and revisor of *Between Pacific Tides* (third and fourth editions); has received professional recognition by serving on a host of national committees, as a guest lecturer, and as president of several professional organizations.

LISCA, PETER. Associate Professor of English, University of Florida; author of *The Wide World of John Steinbeck;* Smith-Mundt Professor of American Literature at the University of Zargosa, Spain; consultant and participant in the USIA film, *John Steinbeck;* published in *Modern Language Notes, PMLA, Twentieth Century Literature, Modern Fiction Studies, College English, Western Humanities Review, Philological Quarterly.*

METZGER, CHARLES R. Professor of English, University of Southern California; Fulbright Professor of American Literature, San Paulo, Brazil. Author of a monograph on Thoreau and Whitman and another on Emerson and Greenough; published in *Annals of Science, Western Humanities Review, Midwest Quarterly, Modern Fiction Studies, Emerson Society Quarterly, Personalist, Coranto, Academus, Walt Whitman Review.*

MORSBERGER, ROBERT M. Associate Professor of English, California State Polytechnic at Pomona; author of *James Thurber* in the Twayne U. S. Authors Series, two composition books published by T. Y. Crowell; U.S.A.I.D. advisor to University of Nigeria, Nsukka, published articles in various scholarly journals.

SHIVELY, CHARLES. Senior in English, Oregon State University; American literature major who is now a graduate student at the University of Washington, Seattle.

STREET, WEBSTER. Attorney-at-law, Monterey, California; long-time friend of John Steinbeck.

EDITORS

ASTRO, RICHARD. Assistant Professor of English, Oregon State University; coordinator of the 1970 Steinbeck Conference; published in *Modern Fiction Studies, American Literature Abstracts, Twentieth Century Literature, Steinbeck Quarterly;* recently appointed as Assistant Editor of the *Steinbeck Quarterly* in the academic year of 1970-1971.

HAYASHI, TETSUMARO. Assistant Professor of English, Ball State University; Editor of the *Steinbeck Quarterly;* founder and director of the John Steinbeck Society of America; general editor of the Steinbeck Monograph Series; author of *John Steinbeck: A Concise Bibliography* (1967), *Sketches of American Culture* (1960), *Arthur Miller Criticism* (1969), *A Textual Study of A Looking Glasse for London* (1969); published articles in the U.S.A., India, and Japan; currently publishing *A Looking Glasse for London and England, an Elizabethan Text* (1970) and *Robert Greene Criticism* (1970 or 1971).

INDEX